Introduction by James Marston Fitch
Catalog by Ise Gropius

Circulated by the
International Exhibitions Foundation
1972–1974

Catalog text: Ise Gropius. Technical data for the buildings from 1948 to 1965 was partly taken from the book *The Architects Collaborative, Inc.*, A. Niggli, Ltd., Teufen, Switzerland. The text was edited by the Massachusetts Institute of Technology Press, Cambridge, Massachusetts.
Cover: An isometric drawing by Herbert Bayer of Walter Gropius's studio in the Bauhaus, Dessau.
Catalog design: Designs & Devices, Boston, Massachusetts.
Printer: The Meriden Gravure Company, Meriden, Connecticut.

Library of Congress catalog card number: 78-152340
ISBN: 0262 57023 8 (paperback)

Foreword

Introduction

The project for an exhibition of the lifework of Walter Gropius was made possible through the participation of many private and public contributors. I want to take this opportunity to express my sincere gratitude to those who have helped in the complicated task of recording the sixty-three years of his architectural productivity.

The incentive to undertake such a project came from the members of The Architects' Collaborative (TAC), with whom Walter Gropius had been associated for twenty-four years. They had assembled a collection of works that Gropius had designed and personally supervised, and these were circulated in American architectural schools. Upon request, the collection was finally enlarged to include work done since 1928, the year when he left the Bauhaus in Dessau. The augmented collection was then exhibited by the Galleria d'Arte del Naviglio in Milan, and travelled from there to Athens, Nicosia and Darmstadt.

When requests came from other European cities to show the whole of the architectural work of Walter Gropius, I asked for and received a grant from the Graham Foundation for Advanced Studies in the Fine Arts, Chicago, Illinois, to extend the preparatory work to the year 1906, and to plan a detailed catalog. The German and English texts of the catalog entries were assembled by myself in consultation with members of TAC and under the editorial guidance of the Massachusetts Institute of Technology Press.

The first version of this retrospective exhibition travels in Europe, sponsored and organized by the Bauhaus-Archiv, formerly in Darmstadt, and now in Berlin, Germany.

The second version has now been prepared for America, where Gropius spent so many important years of his life, and where there has been much demand for a thorough survey of his work. The exhibition is circulated under the auspices of the International Exhibitions Foundation, Washington, D. C. I wish to thank Mrs. John A. Pope, President of the Foundation, and Miss Pamela Worden, Executive Assistant, for their cooperation in presenting this exhibition to students, architects and laymen throughout the country.

Ise Gropius
Lincoln, Massachusetts

This first comprehensive survey of the life work of Walter Gropius can only serve to confirm his international reputation. For the buildings shown here demonstrate two notable facts about his *oeuvre;* its astonishing consistency, when viewed across the reach of two-thirds of a century; and its sheer stylistic durability. Both of these qualities are remarkable, considering the tumultuous decades which they spanned and the telescoped historical process under which they developed.

This viability of Gropius' architecture is not at all accidental. To the contrary, it is the consequence of ethical and esthetic goals which he set for himself quite early and from which he very seldom (and never seriously) deviated throughout a long and active career. This viability is obvious no matter from what point of departure one chooses to analyze the corpus of his work. That the design of the Chicago Tribune Tower of 1922 should so closely resemble that of the Gropiusstadt of 1970 speaks eloquently of the internal esthetic equilibrium of Gropius as a designer. But that both of them could be equally *au courant* in purely stylistic terms today is even more remarkable, in exactly the same way that fifty-year-old compositions by Picasso or Stravinsky strike us as being completely contemporary. This is the quality which establishes Walter Gropius as one of the creators of Twentieth Century vision.

Gropius not only believed that the complexity of modern life demanded a collaborative effort on the part of architects, artists, town planners and engineers. He also practiced in this fashion, whenever the conditions of life warranted it. Thus the first 15 years of his professional life was marked by a close association with Adolph Meyer who worked for him as his 'Chef Architekt', a position Gropius had himself held in the Peter Behrens office. In England he went into partnership with Maxwell Fry during the years 1934–1937; and with his former Bauhaus colleague Marcel Breuer during the early years in Cambridge, Massachusetts (1938–1941). And of course the last twenty-four years of his life were spent as a fully active member of 'The Architects Collaborative'.

This collaborative activity of Gropius inevitably means that the exact degree of his participation in the design of a given building is not always entirely clear. (In TAC, as in the case of all big offices, men other than the principals could play important roles in design decisions.) But the esthetic congruity of the buildings here exhibited is alone enough to establish his primacy as a form-giver; and what was almost certainly the finest building of his whole career—the Bauhaus at Dessau—was designed during one of those periods when he was practicing alone, without collaborators. In any case, the whole issue of authorship hinges on one of the most fundamental theses of his life—namely, that the task facing modern architects was the creation of a supra-personal idiom, one purged of subjectivism and idiosyncrasy and hence available to all architects in the solution of the widest range of social problems.

Unlike his contemporaries, Mies and LeCorbusier, Gropius's prestige as an architect has always been closely linked to that of a teacher. Despite the fact that he spent only nine of his eighty-six years at the Bauhaus, he was always identified with this extraordinary institution (of which, like Jefferson at Charlottesville, he was designer of both curriculum and campus). This identification often weighed heavily upon Gropius

in later years, because it compelled him to spend both time and energy in explaining and defending it before a profession which—while fluctuating between admiration and hostility—was never neutral. It was not that he ever had occasion to regret the Bauhaus or its accomplishments. It was rather that, like most great creators, he aspired to be a practitioner more than to be a teacher. In his own perspective of his life he felt his architectural work to be the more important of the two: and his two terms as a teacher, first at Dessau and later at Cambridge, he regarded as being, in a certain sense, interruptions in his task.

Like those other seminal architects of this century—Wright, Mies and LeCorbusier—Gropius also was the victim of a very special historical circumstance. These men were the indisputable creators of the esthetic idiom of their times: yet they lived on to become old men, continuing to practice in the context of unprecedented ebb and flow of style and taste. Thus they had the experience of being at once the almost mythic founders of a classic style and the actual practitioners of it—in competition, so to say, with their grandsons. This odd historic situation undoubtedly exacerbated the normal friction between generations. In recent years it has become almost de rigeur for the sons and grandsons to denigrate the rationalism of the Bauhaus ethic, the functionalism of the Gropian esthetic, as being old-hat, irrelevant, out-of-date. If this were truly the case, then how is one to explain today, the contemporaneity of the Kallenbach house of 1922 or of the summer house on the Baltic of 1924? If Bauhausian functionalism were indeed an error, then how is one to explain the appalling decline in industrial design between the Adler cabriolet of 1930 and the Thunderbird of

1971? or between the interior design of Gropius' own office at the Bauhaus and the motel decor of American architecture in the Seventies? The lesson of this exhibition would seem to be that, while we may have copied Bauhaus forms too glibly, we have studied Gropian principles not at all: for the noble gravity of the architecture here on display —sober, timeless, technically flawless—is precisely the expression of these principles.

If this exhibition does nothing more than to persuade the current generation of architectural students to re-examine the heritage which Walter Gropius has bequeathed them, it will have fulfilled its purpose.

James Marston Fitch
Columbia University
New York, N. Y.

Biographical data

1883	Born on May 18 in Berlin, Germany to Walter and Manon (née Scharnweber) Gropius.
1903/07	Studied architecture at the Universities of Berlin and Munich. Travelled and worked in Spain.
1908/10	Chief Assistant to Professor Peter Behrens, Berlin.
1910	Private architectural practice.
1914/18	Participation in the First World War, on the western front.
1919	Director of the Grossherzoglich-Sachsen-Weimarische Hochschule für Angewandte Kunst and of the Grossherzogliche Kunstakademie in Weimar (The Grand Ducal School of Applied Art and The Grand Ducal Academy of Art); these two schools he united under the name "Staatliches Bauhaus Weimar"
1925	Continued as Director of the above institute, which he moved to Dessau, Anhalt and renamed "Bauhaus Dessau."
1928	Resumed private practice in Berlin. Visited the U.S.A.
1934/37	Private practice in London, England, in partnership with the British architect Maxwell Fry.
1937	Professor of Architecture at the Graduate School of Design, Harvard University, Cambridge, Massachusetts.
1938/41	Private practice in partnership with Marcel Breuer.
1938/52	Chairman of the Department of Architecture, Graduate School of Design, Harvard University.
1945	Formed "The Architects Collaborative," Cambridge, Massachusetts.
1969	Died on July 5 in Boston, Massachusetts.

Walter Gropius discussing the design for Gropiusstadt with Alex Cvijanovic (left) and Royston Daley
(right), 1966.

Buildings, Plans, Projects

*• Indicates building or project is illustrated in
this catalog.*

1
• HOUSING FOR FARM WORKERS, 1906
• FARM SERVICE BUILDING, 1906
Janikow Estate, Dramburg, Pomerania
Architect: Walter Gropius
Client: Erich Gropius, Walter Gropius's uncle

TWO-FAMILY HOUSE, 1906
Dramburg, Pomerania
Architect: Walter Gropius
Client: A neighbor of Erich Gropius

When, at the age of twenty-three, Walter
Gropius was entrusted with the design of workmen's
housing and farm buildings on the Pomeranian
estate of his uncle, Erich Gropius, he was faced for
the first time with a problem that was to become a
lifetime concern for him: housing for low-income
groups.

Although the job to be done in Janikow had an
entirely feudal basis — a big landowner showing
paternal concern for the welfare of his workers — it
is probable that Gropius's ideas on the mass production of housing through prefabrication, which
emerged as a full-fledged plan four years later, first
took shape in these surroundings. It was made
clear to him that it would become increasingly
unrealistic to attempt to solve the financial problems of housing by relying on the sporadic initiative
of well-meaning developers and on the use of traditional craftsman's techniques in building.

2
• FAGUS SHOE-LAST FACTORY, 1911
Alfeld, Germany
Architect: Walter Gropius with Adolf Meyer
Client: Karl Benscheidt

In 1908 Walter Gropius left the architectural
office of Peter Behrens, his great teacher, to open
his own office. While scouting around for work, he
received an interesting offer to build a new factory
for Karl Benscheidt, the owner of a shoe-last factory
in Alfeld an der Leine. Benscheidt had already
received a finished site plan, floor plans and
construction proposals for a new factory from the
architect Eduard Werner, but felt that the building
should be improved by a well-designed façade. For
this job he commissioned Gropius, who entered the
design phase when the foundations had already
been laid. Through patient persuasion Gropius
managed to bring his client around to his own way
of doing things, and finally in 1911 the construction
was begun according to Gropius's specifications.
With the help of a loan from the United States (the
United Shoe Machinery Corporation), the buildings
were finished that same year. *

By giving architectural expression to the trend
towards transparency and weightlessness, the
duality between architecture and construction
techniques that had persisted throughout the nineteenth century was resolved for the first time.

Structural data: The windows are obviously the
determining feature of the main building. It was the
first true use of a curtain-wall; through the use of
cantilevered steel-frame construction, the wall
becomes a mere screen stretched between the
upright columns of the framework. The building
inspectors demanded that the window balustrades
be reinforced with brick, and the client also hesitated
at first about the suspended glass front and the
missing corner supports. Calculations showed,
however, that a considerable economic gain could
be obtained by using this construction method
rather than the traditional one, and the client took

the risk. His decision was probably also strongly
influenced by his social concern for the welfare of
his workmen and by his realization that they would
benefit from the well-lighted interior of their work
spaces.

—————————
*Helmut Weber, *Walter Gropius und das
Faguswerk*. Callway Verlag, 1961.

3
• BENZENE MOTOR COACH, 1913
Designer: Walter Gropius
Client: Königsberg Locomotive Works

Engine and sleeping car. Anticipated the principle of the diesel-driven car, which came into general use much later.

4
GERMAN RAILWAY CAR COMPARTMENTS, 1914
Designer: Walter Gropius
Client: Deutsche Reichsbahn

Shown at the Werkbund Exhibition in Cologne,
1914.

5
• WERKBUND EXHIBITION MODEL FACTORY, 1914
(Office building, machine shop & pavilion)
Cologne, Germany
Architect: Walter Gropius with Adolf Meyer
Client: Der Deutsche Werkbund

The Deutsche Werkbund, founded in 1907 by a
group of industrial leaders, architects, artists, crafts-
men and their spokesmen, pursued the aim of
encouraging higher standards in the design of
manufactured goods through collaboration between

these groups. In their influential exhibitions they tried to educate the public by demonstrating desirable new developments through practical examples.

The Cologne exhibition, though interrupted by the outbreak of the First World War, was a high point in their endeavors because of the very unusual buildings erected there for public viewing. Some of them had originated in the studio of Gropius, but these buildings, which generated so much excitement, have only survived in the form of photographs and magazine articles, since like all the others they were torn down at the close of the exhibition.

The task Gropius had set for himself was to show a medium-sized manufacturing plant with its auxiliary buildings. To carry this plan through successfully he had to solicit contributions from local industry. What emerged was an office building with adjacent open garages in steel frame construction (later to be called 'carports') and, separated from the office building by a large court, a manufacturing hall with a broad three-part central nave, a keel-shaped roof, and curved skylights.

The glass-walled office building even extended the glass curtain around the corners. The entrance side, a windowless wall of bricklike, buff-colored limestone with narrow slits, was flanked by two glassed-in spiral stairways leading to the roof terrace. Here two superstructures rising from each end, with widely cantilevered overhangs, were planned as dance floors, with a covered restaurant connecting them.

"The effect of the whole was grandiose — a lay temple of symphonic symmetry, a hall in which the machine and the building, the one wholly, the other in part, of metal, celebrated a new reconciliation. Here utilitarian architecture, aided by the element of spectacular display, takes on a dignity and beauty through its own high, fearless honesty, the frank, graceful avowal of its purpose."*

---
*Herman Scheffauer, "The Work of Walter Gropius," *The Architectural Review*, London, Winter 1923.

6
SOMMERFELD RESIDENCE, 1921
Berlin-Dahlem, Germany
Architect: Walter Gropius with Adolf Meyer
Client: Adolf Sommerfeld

The great scarcity of good building material after the First World War caused the client, a prom-

inent contractor, to purchase a dismantled navy ship in order to use the teakwood for his house. The Bauhaus workshops were employed for part of the furnishings and for decorating the house.

7
OTTE RESIDENCE, 1921/22
Berlin-Zehlendorf, Germany
Architect: Walter Gropius with Adolf Meyer
Client: Herr Otte

8
MONUMENT, 1922
Weimar, Germany
Architect: Walter Gropius
Client: Labor Unions of Weimar

This monument was erected in memory of those who perished during the struggle to avert the coup d'état by the right-wing politician, Wolfgang Kapp (Kapp Putsch) in Germany in 1920. The concrete monument was dynamited in 1933 and replaced by a Nazi symbol. In 1946 it was reconstructed from photographs, with some deviations from the original design, and placed on the original site.

9
• **CHICAGO TRIBUNE BUILDING, 1922**
Chicago, Illinois
Competition Project
Architect: Walter Gropius with Adolf Meyer
Client: The Chicago Tribune

Typically summing up what was expected of the architect of that time was the following remark in the program for the competition: "It is unnecessary for the purpose of this competition to know the mechanical needs of the Chicago Tribune or to be concerned with the plans for developing and extending the various departments which will occupy space in the new building. The purpose and desire constituting this competition is to secure primarily a distinctive and beautiful exterior design."

Two hundred and sixty-three entries were submitted. The winning design was by John Mead Howells and Raymond M. Hood. The jury, oblivious of the achievements of the "Chicago School" which had been inspired by Louis Sullivan and Frank Lloyd Wright, had chosen to return to Beaux-Arts standards and by this decision temporarily turned the clock

back on the American development of a truly contemporary architecture.

10
• **KALLENBACH RESIDENCE, 1922**
Berlin, Germany
Project
Architect: Walter Gropius with Adolf Meyer
Client: Herr Kallenbach

11
MODEL FOR STANDARDIZED HOUSES, 1923
Weimar, Germany
Project of the Bauhaus Architectural Department
Directed by Walter Gropius

Model for a series of houses representing variations of the same basic house-units. By adding to the individual units, and rearranging them into different groupings, houses of different sizes and appearances could be assembled, thereby resolving the contradictory demands for standardization and variability.

12
• **MUNICIPAL THEATER, 1922**
Jena, Germany
Architect: Walter Gropius with Adolf Meyer
Client: The City of Jena

This theater came about as a result of a commission to renovate a primitive entertainment hall with exposed rafters, which for economic reasons had to be used if the town was to have a theater at all.

The total absence of decoration on the exterior of the building, which consists of very carefully proportioned cubistic masses within and without, disconcerted the early visitors. Another cause for consternation were the large areas of pure, bold color, without any ornamentation. In spite of this, contemporary reviews show that the unadorned, noble forms did not fail to make their impact, and the citizens of Jena were astounded by the transition this building had undergone, from a humdrum structure to one displaying a new architectural spirit, different from anything they had ever seen before.

The theater, which seated 750 persons, was situated in a small landscaped court away from the street. Its front showed a broad, white, totally unstructured center part, extended by two parallel recessed wings with beveled corners, the whole elevated upon a long plinth. The roofline showed no mouldings and was perceived as a sharp, straight line against the sky, but this line actually consisted of a taut curve with an increase of six inches in the middle to prevent the roofline from having a sunken appearance, a device which was already in use in ancient Greece and India. Outside as well as inside, the individual building elements were not simply put next to each other or joined by a connecting link, but they interpenetrated each other in a dynamic fashion.

The ceiling of the auditorium descends toward the side walls in a series of horizontal projections that recede at some distance from the facing wall. With this design device the Renaissance principle of enclosing the ceiling within a frame is definitely abandoned. Instead, the stage is almost invaded by these protruding forms, which carry the eye forward and create the impression that the open scene has become incorporated with the auditorium to form one unified space.

Thus, under the most stringent conditions and at a time when many German theaters had to close for lack of funds, a new challenge to stage and theater design was successfully met.

13

INTERNATIONAL ACADEMY OF PHILOSOPHY, 1924
Erlangen, Germany
Project
Architect: Walter Gropius with Adolf Meyer
Client: Professor Hofmann

With the founding of an international philosophical academy, an ambitious plan was to be realized, which would offer qualified scholars from all over the world the opportunity to work on their projects in congenial surroundings and with access to excellent libraries. The financing of this project through contributions from various interested countries had already been initiated, and the membership list included the names of eminent professors from England, America, Italy, China and Sweden. Gropius himself participated in the formulation of the building program.

The purpose of the building was to create a serene environment, conducive to contemplation, intellectual exchange and enlightenment. It was to be, in so far as possible, a self-contained entity,

offering all the facilities required for effective scholarly research. It also was to play an active role in community affairs and provided space to facilitate this. Designed two years earlier than the Bauhaus building in Dessau, it already shows a similar space conception.

Unfortunately, the initiator of the idea, a member of the faculty of the University of Erlangen, encountered so many insurmountable obstacles in procuring the necessary funds that the plan had to be given up.

14

• SUMMER HOUSE BY THE BALTIC SEA, 1924
Project
Architect: Walter Gropius with Adolf Meyer
Client: Herr von Klitzing

15

TEACHERS' ASSOCIATION BUILDING, 1925
Dresden, Germany
Project
Architect: Walter Gropius
Client: Dresden Teachers' Association

One of the problems of this project was its location on property flanked by other buildings. The solution was to face the building inward onto a court opening onto the street.

The program called for a theater designed for the use of members of the Association as well as other organizations. The restaurant was to be open to the public. There were to be many meeting rooms for clubs and groups specializing in different educational fields. Teacher-training classrooms, a model classroom, exhibition space, library and offices were also provided.

16

• THE BAUHAUS BUILDING, 1925
Dessau, Germany
Architect: Walter Gropius
Client: The City of Dessau

The Bauhaus Building was commissioned by the City of Dessau, under the direction of its foresighted mayor, Fritz Hesse. Construction was begun in 1925 and the building was dedicated in 1926.

The building occupied an area of about 28,300 square feet, with an approximate volume of

1,150,000 cubic feet. The total cost amounted to $230,000. The Bauhaus consisted of a workshop building, the Trade School, an auditorium with stage and dining hall, and a studio tower.

The laboratory workshops contained a basement with printing plant, dye-works, sculpture room, packing and storage rooms, janitor's quarters and furnaces; a ground floor with carpentry shop, exhibition rooms and a large vestibule, leading to an auditorium with raised stage; a second floor with weaving workshop, rooms for the preliminary course and a large lecture room; a third floor with wall-painting workshop, and two lecture halls that could be connected to make one large exhibition hall.

The Trade School contained classrooms and administrative quarters, instructors' rooms, library, physics hall, and model shops.

The bridge connecting the Trade School with the workshop building contained administration offices on the first floor and, on the second, the architectural department and private architectural offices of Walter Gropius.

The auditorium was connected with the studio wing (containing students' quarters and facilities). The stage, situated between the auditorium and the dining hall, could be opened on both sides, so that spectators could sit on either side. For gala occasions all walls surrounding the stage could be removed and the space occupied by dining hall, stage, auditorium and vestibule could be combined into one large hall. The dining hall was connected with the kitchen, and with a spacious terrace which led to the sports areas.

The adjoining student dormitories consisted of 28 combined study and sleeping rooms on five floors, each with a kitchenette. The basement contained baths, exercise rooms with dressing alcoves and an electrically equipped laundry.

The building showed efficient circulation patterns, a clearly recognizable separation of the different parts of the whole, and enough flexibility for possible reassignment of room uses. It had no clearly defined frontal façade and thus could not be grasped from any single viewpoint. It differed radically from the strictly symmetrical appearance of the conventional public buildings of its time.

The interior decoration of the entire building was done by the students of the wall-painting workshop. The design and execution of all lighting fixtures of the assembly hall, dining room and studios was handled by the students of the metal workshop. The tubular steel furniture of the assembly hall, dining room and studios was made from designs by Marcel Breuer. Lettering was executed by the printing workshop.

Structural data: reinforced concrete frame with mushroom columns in the basement, brick masonry, hollow tile floors. The flat roofs were covered with asphalt sheets over torfoleum insulation and could be walked upon. The roofs were drained by cast-iron pipes running down through the building. Exterior finish of the building was cement stucco, painted with mineral paint.

17

• **HOUSES FOR BAUHAUS FACULTY, 1925/26**
Dessau, Germany
Architect: Walter Gropius
Client: The City of Dessau

One detached house without a studio and three semidetached duplexes, each unit having a large studio, are set on a sparsely wooded site not far from the Bauhaus building.

The six dwellings in the three duplexes are identical yet different in appearance. The floor plan of one of the two units is the mirror image of its semidetached neighbor turned by 90 degrees.

This arrangement demonstrates a theory of construction that preoccupied Gropius throughout his life. The theory involved the creation of identical units that can be assembled or combined in a great number of ways, so that the final product has an intrinsic flexibility and a variety of external appearances. A combination of the greatest possible standardization with the greatest possible versatility.

Structural data: The foundation was of concrete and the walls composed of cinder blocks. The reinforced concrete skeleton was partly cantilevered to form loggias. The roof, on which it was possible to walk, was covered by artificial stone slabs over a gravel mixture base.

18

• **TÖRTEN DEVELOPMENT, 1926/28**
Dessau, Germany
Architect: Walter Gropius
Client: The City of Dessau

In contrast to many housing plans for low-income groups which turn out after completion to be far above the financial means of their prospective

owners, these houses were actually attainable for the unskilled workman's family. This was achieved by a very comprehensive "critical path programming," a time and labor saving method which provided for the smooth assembly-line production of the building units at the site. In the construction period of 1928, 130 houses were finished within 88 days, including the fabrication of hollow cinder blocks and all other building parts on the site, and finished plastering inside and out.

The 316 single-family houses with four or five rooms were organized for semirural living, each unit placed on a 3767 sq. ft. site. They were centrally heated and each house was provided with bathroom facilities. The cooperative building contained, in addition to shops at street level, 3 floors of dwellings, each with 3 rooms and kitchen.

Structural data: designed on a modular basis to simplify its standardized construction, only the reinforced concrete beams and cinder blocks for the load-bearing crosswalls were cast on the site.

19

• **PREFABRICATED HOUSE FOR WERKBUND HOUSING EXHIBITION, 1927**
Stuttgart, Germany
Architect: Walter Gropius
Client: The City of Stuttgart

After his firxt experiences with serial housing in Törten near Dessau, Walter Gropius was asked by the Werkbund Exhibit Committee to contribute two buildings for the Weissenhofsiedlung in Stuttgart. The Württemberg Chapter of the German Werkbund succeeded in persuading the Stuttgart administration to permit construction of sixty permanent dwellings of an experimental character as part of a municipal housing program.

Mies van der Rohe was commissioned with the overall planning and direction of the project and sixteen avant-garde architects from five European countries were asked to contribute.

This exhibition became a first demonstration of the common aims of modern architects who up to then had worked in isolation. The plan was to respond to demands of prospective house owners with an offer of different house-types to provide maximum economic advantage and present a whole new approach to living. Since experimentation was the crucial point, each house-type was built only once. The house shown here was

Gropius's contribution to the problem of producing the industrially manufactured single-family dwelling, assembled in a dry process with only the concrete floor slab constructed at the site.

Gropius wrote about it: "For the two experimental house projects designed by me for the Weissenhofsiedlung, I have set for myself the goal of finding new solutions for the prefabricated house. In trying to bring down the price for the housing of middle- and low-income groups, we succeeded in erecting an economically acceptable series of houses through the use of big building machines at the site. To use this procedure for the building of single-family dwellings would be uneconomical because of the high cost of the machines. To satisfy the strong demand for industrially mass-produced, but individually deliverable houses, new procedures have to be developed — and this is what I tried to show in my experiment."[*]

Structural data: Cast-in-place concrete floor slab. Light steel frame skeleton with walls of compressed cork faced with asbestos cement panels. Inner facing of plywood.

[*] "Stuttgarter Beiträge", No. 4, 1968

20

• **TOTAL THEATER, 1927**
Berlin, Germany
Project
Architect: Walter Gropius
Client: Erwin Piscator

In a speech at the Volta Congress in Rome in 1934 Walter Gropius dealt with the problems of the theater and stated that "the task of the theater architect of today, as I see it, is to create a great and flexible instrument that will respond in terms of light and space to every requirement of the stage director, an instrument so impersonal that it never restrains him from giving full play to his vision and imagination, a building whose spatial treatment stimulates and refreshes the human spirit. . . . The shape of the stage and its orientation to the spectators is of utmost importance for the development of the dramatic action and the effect this has on the senses. This must be the starting point of the new conception of theatrical space.

"The ground plan for this theater, which was developed according to the demands of Erwin Piscator, the director, is elliptical and its section a parabolic curve, in keeping with the requirements of good acoustics. It resembles an egg cut in half lengthwise, with a deep tripartite stage at one end. The orchestra seats, arranged amphitheatrically, are not bordered by boxes but encircle, pincerlike, the circular proscenium which can be raised or lowered. This stage is at the same time built off center into a larger turntable that holds the first rows of spectators. An actor can descend into the audience or mount the stage in any number of ways. Three circular aisles through and around the theater can be used for demonstrations and processions. The first of these surrounds the proscenium stage, the second the large turntable, and the third runs around the whole auditorium behind the interior columns supporting the building.

"A complete transformation of the theater takes place when the large turntable is turned 180° The proscenium stage then becomes an arena in the center of the auditorium, surrounded by spectators on all sides. Actors can enter this arena either from below or from the aisle leading back to the main stage, or from above by ladders or similar apparatus to be lowered from the ceiling.

"Thus the project provides a stage in arena form, a proscenium stage and a three-partite backstage. If desired, the transformation can take place even during a performance. This thrusts the spectator physically into another spatial context and makes him an active participant in the action. Special attention was given to Piscator's demand that projectors and screens be put everywhere, to replace the scenery during an arena performance. Screens stretched between the twelve columns surrounding the amphitheater can have films projected from the rear, so that the scenic background draws the spectator more completely into the drama, while the action on the stage holds him captive. There is no distinction between the stage and the auditorium; it is a three-dimensional space instead of a flat 'stage-picture' and the creation of a projection space instead of a projection screen."*

The expenditures for such a flexible stage mechanism would be fully justified by the diversity of purposes to which this transformable building would lend itself: the presentation of drama, opera, film, dance, choral or instrumental music, sports events, or mass meetings. This should make it of interest to cities unable to build and maintain separate structures for each of these enterprises.

---

*Walter Gropius, "Theaterbau," in *Convegno di*

lettere, Oct. 1934. Reale Accademia d'Italia, Rome, 1935, p. 160.

21
• 'STADTKRONE,' 1928
(Cultural and sports center)
Halle a.d. Saale, Germany
Project
Architect: Walter Gropius
Client: The City of Halle

The peculiar site selected for the group of buildings called for in the program of the City of Halle — a high bluff overlooking the Saale River, rising out of a wide plain — demanded a spectacular and imaginative solution. Gropius met this challenge by giving the big auditorium building a silhouette which made it the focal point of the whole design. The commanding height of the building was achieved without excessive expenditures by means of platforms, accessible from stairs and elevators, above the vaulted dome of the auditorium. Equipped with restaurant and cafe, the landscaped grounds were to be a special point of attraction and at the same time, offer a marvelous scenic view to the public. The unusual topography was to be emphasized by having the various levels of the terrain and of the platforms covered with plants to give the impression of hanging gardens.

Particular care was given to the problem of easy filling and emptying of the big auditorium. The whole building rests on a column grid which provides very spacious cloakrooms underneath the hall, accessible from all sides. The shape of the auditorium resulted from thorough acoustical studies. Since the great shell is covered and protected by the garden platform, it was possible to construct it from relatively light material, so that it could be hung instead of being supported from the ground. This meant it could be shaped according to considerations of acoustics rather than of structure. In the choice of material, Gropius preferred steel and glass which, through their respective lightness and transparency, lent themselves to more unusual and innovative construction methods.

The museum is located next to the lecture hall, the library and the reading rooms, so that the public is motivated to use the building frequently.

The sports forum at some distance was planned for a maximum of 30,000 spectators. It has direct underground access to the gymnasium; adjoining it is a dormitory for athletes.

22
ZUCKERKANDL COUNTRY HOUSE, 1927/28
Jena, Germany
Architect: Walter Gropius
Client: Herr Zuckerkandl

23
• MUNICIPAL EMPLOYMENT OFFICE, 1927/28
Dessau, Germany
Architect: Walter Gropius
Client: The City of Dessau

The problem here was to find a ground plan which would do justice to the specific requirements of this new type of building. Applications for employment from a large number of job seekers were to be processed by a small number of functionaries. This resulted in the semicircular shape of the building. Individual interview rooms were located in the interior. The fluctuating demand for space could be satisfied by rearranging the dividing partitions.

The Bauhaus carpentry shop supplied the furniture; the Bauhaus metal-working shop made the lighting fixtures; the color scheme for each room was carried out by the wall-painting studio.

Structural data: The actual structure is based on a steel skeleton; the walls are covered with buff facing bricks. Window sashes are of steel.

24
• DAMMERSTOCK HOUSING DEVELOPMENT,
1927/28
Karlsruhe, Germany
Architect: Walter Gropius
Client: The City of Karlsruhe

Gropius's scheme for a housing development on a site near the city of Karlsruhe won first prize in a competition. He developed the site plan and acted as coordinator for eight architects commissioned to design portions of the development. The 228 units built in 1927 were only a third of the whole project. Each subsequent addition was to take advantage of the latest experiences and improvements in the field of housing.

The buildings were located so as to provide both east and west exposure, to secure an equal amount of sun and an unobstructed view of the Black Forest for every inhabitant. Rows of four-story apartment blocks were placed along the eastern side of the tract and served as a barrier to noise and dust entering from the principal roadway. Vehicular traffic within the complex was handled by two streets running east-west. Two sidewalks bisected these streets and provided access to individual unit entrances. Flower gardens and lawns were placed between houses and sidewalks. In all there were 23 different housing types offered. The variety of solutions arrived at for practically equal unit sizes present an excellent basis for comparison.

The buildings designed by Gropius consisted of a five-story apartment block with 4½ room apartments, a four-story apartment block with outside access galleries, and some single-family row houses.

The structural specifications set by Gropius to ensure economical construction and a harmonius and consistent appearance of the buildings were: flat roofs, uniform story heights, equal window units.

25
• **MODULAR FURNITURE UNITS, 1927/29**
Designer: Walter Gropius
Client: Feder Stores, Berlin

This type of furniture was designed with the low-income family in mind. Standard elements could be arranged side by side, or in various combinations, in order to obtain maximum use.

26
• **MEGASTRUCTURE, 1928**
Project
Architect: Walter Gropius

At the time of its conception this utopian project was an attempt to visualize the housing needs of the future. Meanwhile the 'future' has overtaken us, while no really far-reaching changes in the organization of society or in our planning for the housing of the rising population have been made. This early attempt to face the problems of the future anticipates a solution similar to our present idea of megastructures.

The section through the megastructure, or 'Wohnberg,' shows the access to the rapid-transit lines connecting the structure with the general transportation system and the internal pedestrian ways between floors at different levels.

The arrangement of the floor plans for the

living units shows that a total change in the social order was visualized by Gropius, a change that would bring about equality of the sexes and would make the *individual* the basic cell of the state, rather than the *family*. He assumed that in such a future development the economy of the rental market would have to be based on the income of the individual rather than on the income of the head of a family. The raising and education of children might then no longer be an isolated experience but part of a communal undertaking. So, one whole floor of this structure is reserved for children's activities and day-care facilities.

Structural data: The steel skeleton carries the prefabricated living units which, through their mass production, can be kept at a low price.

27
• **SLAB APARTMENT BLOCK, 1929**
Project
Architect: Walter Gropius

The multistory apartment blocks proposed by Gropius consisted of narrow rectangular slabs eight to twelve stories high and only one apartment deep. They were not supposed to line the main street but to stand at right angles to it to avoid a corridor effect. Only minor roads connect the buildings, which are separated by large landscaped areas and offer each inhabitant an equal amount of sunlight.

The principal idea of these tall narrow blocks was to loosen the structure of the city by creating new free, open spaces while retaining the same overall population density. At the third congress of CIAM* in Brussels in 1930, Gropius noted: "The city needs to reassert itself. It needs the stimulus resulting from a development of housing peculiarly its own, a type which will combine a maximum of air, sunlight, and open parkland with a minimum of communication roads and maintenance costs. Such conditions can be fulfilled by the multistory apartment block, and consequently its development should be one of the urgent tasks of city planning."

Between 1928 and 1931, Gropius examined the various aspects of the high-rise slab. Questions of sunlight, of better ground use, of financial soundness were developed in comparative schemes entered for large competitions. However, no slab apartment block was erected in Germany at that time. There were many reasons for this: practical problems of financing; the lack of precedent for the use of new structural methods such as steel skele-

tons for apartment houses; the reluctance of owners to introduce elevators into working-class housing and, by no means least important, the attitude of the public. The slab block was a new form of dwelling and as such was bound to encounter a strong psychological opposition. The root cause of the objection was the preference of the general public and the builders alike for the kind of massive structures which they associated with the conventional apartment block around an inner court.

—————————
*Congrès Internationaux de l'Architecture Moderne

28
MODEL HOUSING, 1929
Spandau-Haselhorst, Berlin, Germany
Competition project
Architect: Walter Gropius
Structural Engineer: Stefan Fischer
Client: Reichsforschungsgesellschaft für Wirtschaftlichkeit im Wohnungsbau

In 1929 the Government Research Institute for Planning and Housing arranged a national competition to obtain preliminary proposals for the site plan and appropriate housing types for a tract of land near Spandau. The jury had established guidelines which were designed to eliminate inadequate, obsolete points of view, and to direct the work of the architects towards a thorough investigation of the entire housing industry.

The first prize went to Walter Gropius, who had submitted four different plans for the same site. Of these, the fourth plan (D), with its advantageous slab apartment blocks, came closest to his real intentions, although it offered the least chance of being accepted because of the prejudice against high-rise apartment blocks prevailing at that time. The jury stated that "the proposal of Gropius and Fischer by far surpassed the general level by its significant scientific thoroughness." The different plans proposed were:

A. Mixed housing types, two- three- and five-stories, as one-family row houses, or higher apartment blocks. 2811 dwellings, with sleeping capacity for 10,040.

B. Two-story single-family houses, some with bachelor quarters on the upper floor; 3031 dwellings with sleeping capacity for 11,560.

C. Five-story apartment blocks with outside galleries; 4714 dwellings with sleeping capacity for 22,297. Central management and utilities for the entire project.

D. Twelve-story apartment blocks with outside galleries. 4616 dwellings with sleeping capacity for 17,835. Central management and utilities for the entire project. Very broad open areas between the blocks to allow for a parklike development of the whole site in spite of the density of the settlement. In the middle of each block, a kindergarten accessible from the elevators. Roof terrace available for children in the summer. Sigfried Giedion noted twenty-five years later that this proposal (D) ''gave perhaps the decisive impulse for the widespread acceptance of this particular type of urban planning a few years later.''*

_____
*Sigfried Giedion, *Walter Gropius, Work and Teamwork*. Reinhold Publishing Co., New York, 1954.

29
• SIEMENSSTADT HOUSING DEVELOPMENT, 1929
Berlin, Germany
Architect: Walter Gropius
Engineer: Herr Mengeringhausen
Client: Cooperative Organization, Berlin

The master plan by Hans Scharoun proposed the construction of 1800 apartments and a school. The participating architects, Bartning, Forbat, Gropius, Häring, Henning, and Scharoun, each received a segment of the overall development to design. Two-and-a-half and three-and-a-half-room apartments in three four-story blocks were designed by Gropius.

Structural data: Stuccoed brick.

30
ASCHROTT WELFARE CENTER, 1929
Kassel, Germany
Competition Project
Architect: Walter Gropius
Client: The City of Kassel

According to the program, the building was to contain a large and a small hall, at least 32 offices, a public library, a young people's library and service facilities. The prominent site in the old city center, next to the bridge over the Fulda River, demanded consideration of the environment and adaptation to an existing townscape.

The small hall is placed behind the large one. The partition can be pushed behind the gallery to make the whole length of the two halls available for special occasions. The halls are surrounded by a broad glass-enclosed walk which leads to the refreshment room behind the stage.

Reading rooms are located in the spacious first level, away from street noise. The existing terrace is enlarged and a second one extends from the first level towards the river. Under this terrace, where the land slopes away, is a shaded sitting area. The terraces with recessed balconies, and the roof of the office building, provide the opportunity to landscape the whole complex on the side facing the river.

Structural data: Steel skeleton, hollow brick walls. Basement covered with chocolate-brown colored bricks.

31
ASCHROTT HOME FOR THE AGED, 1929
Kassel, Germany
Competition project
Architect: Walter Gropius
Client: The City of Kassel

The home was planned to accommodate about one hundred elderly women who, for a modest fee, would receive full room and board. Facilities included kitchenettes and dining rooms, rooms for social events, a library with a reading room, guest rooms, and offices plus staff quarters. The site was pleasantly located, facing open woodland.

The Gropius proposal consisted of a thorough analysis of the possible spatial arrangement of the building masses, which resulted in the recommendation of Plan No. 8, because it possessed the greatest advantages with respect to sun exposure, view, efficient circulation patterns, quiet living areas and contiguous garden space.

32
• ADLER CABRIOLET, 1930
Designer: Walter Gropius
Client: Adler Automobile Works, Frankfurt/Main

The design for this Adler sports car is testimony to Gropius's interest in the development of industrial forms and in the bridging of the gap between artistic design and technical production. The front seats could be converted into beds by means of collapsing their back rests. This idea was adopted many years later by other automobile manufacturers.

This car design won first prize in a number of national exhibitions.

33
WERKBUND EXHIBIT, 1930
Grand Palais, Salon des Artistes Décorateurs
Paris, France
Architect: Walter Gropius, in collaboration with Marcel Breuer, Herbert Bayer and L. Moholy Nagy
Client: Der Deutsche Werkbund

The Deutsche Werkbund was entrusted by the German government with the first German exhibition in Paris after the First World War. It commissioned Gropius with the design of the exhibition and the selection of the objects to be shown. Gropius organized the project with three former Bauhaus members as a closely cooperating team, with each designer responsible for some particular aspect. The exhibition consisted of a display of the products of German industry, all carefully selected to show a practicable standard for future mass production. The Werkbund Exhibit sought to promote prototypes of good standardized industrial products, and design of communal facilities for a high-rise apartment house.

Part of the available space in the Grand Palais exhibition hall was devoted to rooms representing a community center for the ten-story slab apartment house project which Gropius was then engaged in working out for Berlin.

Sigfried Giedion described Gropius's contribution as follows: ''On approaching the exhibit, one's eye is at once caught by the glass walls of a swimming pool and gymnasium. It seems that Walter Gropius had a very subtle instinct in opening the exhibit with this overture. Gropius was himself responsible for the entrance area with its swimming pool, gymnasium, bar, dance floor, reading and playing corners, library, radio and record nook, and bulletin board. A metal bridge in the form of a ramp rises over the swimming pool, with an open lattice-like construction of galvanized steel.''*

Le Figaro wrote: ''The success of this exhibit in the delicate atmosphere of Paris betokens one thing above all: a belated recognition of the work done by the Bauhaus. The anger and vituperation that has been vented against the Bauhaus for ten years in Germany is here clearly shown to have been due to a deplorable shortsightedness and lack of instinct. This exhibit is less of a leap into the future than it is the culmination of ten years of progress."

*Giedion, Sigfried, *Walter Gropius, Work and Teamwork*. Reinhold Publishing Co., New York, 1954.

34

• UKRAINIAN STATE THEATER, 1930
Kharkov, Ukraine
Competition project
Architect: Walter Gropius
Client: The Ukrainian Soviet Socialist Republic

Sigfried Giedion wrote that, "This project for the Ukrainian State Theater for Kharkov, seating 4000, is without doubt, both in interior and exterior treatment, one of Gropius's most perfectly balanced compositions. . . . If it had been built it would, in many ways, have given a new impulse to the stagnant art of theater design. Although the program did not permit an application of the principle of the 'total theater,' the stage has been made so flexible that it can be reduced to a small surface for intimate scenes, or the action can be transferred at will into a large apron stage projecting into the midst of the audience. A great circular backdrop increases the depth of the stage. Despite the large scale of the building, every seat has good acoustics and a good view: all are oriented directly upon the stage, with the same angle of sight, which compensates for the long distance. The rows of seats form arcs of a circle exactly following the curved line of the stage, and the same curve is repeated by the outer walls.

Above all, the entire project is an architectural achievement with a rare monumental simplicity. The dreamlike vision of the future development, as first demonstrated in the glass encased spiral staircase towers in the Cologne Exhibition building, appears fully developed in the Kharkov Theatre with its segmental, protruding glass screen of the main entrance and the recessed glass curves of the side entrances. The lobby with its free standing ramps and its slender reinforced concrete columns would have become a showpiece of contemporary architecture."*

Structural data: Steel skeleton, including ramps. Walls of light-weight concrete with exterior covering of very light-colored limestone or sandstone. All windows, including large glass expanses, were of plate glass. Interior walls: foyer and auditorium of very light-colored limestone; front walls

are covered with ribbed aluminum plates. Interior doors are aluminum.

*Sigfried Giedion, *Walter Gropius, Work and Teamwork*. Reinhold Publishing Co., New York, 1954.

35

• PREFABRICA⬛⬛⬛⬛ ⬛⬛⬛⬛ ⬛⬛⬛⬛⬛S, 1931
Finow, German⬛
Architect: Wa⬛⬛⬛⬛⬛⬛⬛
Client: Hirsch⬛⬛⬛⬛⬛⬛ ⬛⬛⬛⬛⬛⬛werke A.G., Berlin

In a book by Martin Wagner,* Walter Gropius gives this report on the copper houses: "The fabrication of copper houses on the assembly line, according to a patent held by Förster and Kraft, was developed by me, both as to techniques and with regard to the organization of the process; this was done only after numerous tests, and expert testimony from scientific institutes.

The advantages of such prefabricated, easily assembled houses are as follows: Elimination of all moisture in the building process; light weight of the building parts; independence of seasonal and atmospheric conditions because of the assemblage character; low maintenance costs because of the high-quality building material, which becomes economical through standardized production; a fixed price without subsequent added costs; short delivery terms."

A number of these houses were built as experimental units at Finow near Berlin just before the economic collapse in Germany forced the closing of the firm.

Structural data: Exteriors were prefabricated wall panels of wood frames with aluminum foil insulation. Corrugated copper sheets provided the exterior finish. Interior facing was of 0.5 mm ribbed aluminum sheeting or asbestos cement sheeting. Connections were bolted with batten protection, with the result that no place in the wall acted as heat or cold conductor. The roof ceilings were also well insulated against heat and cold by the addition of aluminum foil against the roof boarding.

The walls were produced in an assembly line process in workshops especially organized for this kind of mass production. They could be shipped in sizes up to the 6 meters (19 ft. 8 in.) length of each unit, with the glazed windows and the doors already in place. In spite of the high insulation capacity — the thermal resistance equals that of

a brick wall 140 cm (55 in.) thick — one square meter of the finished exterior wall weighed only 15 kg. Even very high interior and very low exterior temperatures resulted in no condensation in the insulation layers. The size of the house could be enlarged or decreased by adding or disassembling the standardized units.

*Martin Wagner, *Das Wachsende Haus*. Deutsches Verlagshaus, Munich, 1931.

36

• SOVIET PALACE, 1931
Moscow, USSR
Competition project
Architect: Walter Gropius
Client: The Russian Embassy, Berlin

A number of foreign architects were asked to participate in this competition, including Gropius, Mendelsohn, Poelzig (Germany), Le Corbusier and Perret (France), Jos. Urban & Lamb and G. O. Hamilton (U.S.A.)

The site for this grandiose project was in the heart of old Moscow, on a large site to be created by razing a series of blocks in order to assure easy access and wide visibility. The program called for grouped buildings containing an auditorium to seat 15,000, a vestibule for an additional 14,000, all the necessary auxiliary rooms, and a chamber for the Presidium (300 people) with its own auxiliary rooms. For this group of structures a floor space of 17,000 square meters (180,000 sq. ft.) was to be set aside—this not to include the main auditorium. A second room, to hold 5900, was intended primarily for meetings and conventions but could be converted for use as theater or concert hall. The stage was supposed to hold up to 500 individuals at a time, and provision had to be made for demonstration marches across the stage and through the auditorium. A 500,000 volume library with reading rooms for 200 researchers and exhibition areas amounting to 1500 square meters (16,146 sq. ft.), each with its attendant facilities, were projected. In addition, two rooms each seating 500 and two rooms each seating 200, with a total floor space of 2800 square meters (30,140 sq. ft.) were to be placed in the immediate vicinity. The acoustical and optical problems arising out of such vast dimensions were, of course, formidable.

Gropius conceived this project as "a single gigantic space that could be grasped from a single vantage point, built over a circle as the symbol of the cohesion of the masses in a human and political super-unit. The large circular structure fills the western part of the site, leaving the eastern portion down to the Lenivka River free for mass demonstrations. Access for the public is provided around the periphery, with separate roads for members of the Presidium, the press and the performers. The approach is from the south, exits are to the north. There are direct connections with the projected subway terminal located beneath the Palace. Short paths connect the individual units.

The auditoriums and stages form a single spatial unity, instead of being separated between the real world of the spectator and the theatrical world of make-believe."* The stage machinery was a precision apparatus of technical functualism, impersonal yet adaptable and flexible enough to permit of maximum changeability and horizontal and vertical mobility.

Structural data: The supporting parts of the building were designed as a bearing system of reinforced concrete columns and joists, on which iron roof girders rested for the vaulting of the halls. The entire surfaces between the vertical concrete ribs were to be faced with stones from the different rock formations of the Soviet Union (granite, marble, porphyry, etc.). All the roof surfaces were of sheet copper; the window frames were to have bronze profiles.

*Die Neue Stadt, Vol. 2, Frankfurt/Main. 1932

37
CLUBHOUSE, 1932
Buenos Aires, Argentina
Project
Architect: Walter Gropius

38
NONFERROUS METAL EXHIBITION, 1934
Berlin, Germany
Architect: Walter Gropius with Joost Schmidt
Client: Nonferrous Metal Industry Association

Part of a project for the Nonferrous Metal Manufacturers of Germany. Helix made of a variety of metals and alloys, to turn inside a giant metal drum.

39
HIGH-RISE APARTMENT BLOCKS, 1935
St. Leonard's Hill, Berkshire, England
Project
Architects: Walter Gropius and Maxwell Fry
Client: Isokon, Ltd., London

When Gropius worked with Maxwell Fry in England, they were asked to develop a housing plan for an estate adjacent to the grounds of Windsor Castle and owned by the Duke of Gloucester. In lieu of an earlier plan to divide the magnificent old park into small sites for single-family houses, Gropius and Fry proposed to erect two high-rise blocks of 110 flats and apartments, together with a restaurant, lounge and ballroom. Garages were to be provided out of sight of the main buildings, and a secluded part of the park was to be set aside for a nursery and playground.

Had this plan been carried out, it would have offered a solution to the growing problem of the disposal of large, financially insupportable land-holdings. Although foresighted Englishmen felt that, to combat exploitation, the preservation of the countryside should be given high priority in any policy of development, the scheme remained on paper.

40
LEVY RESIDENCE, 1936
Church Street, Chelsea, London, England
Architects: Walter Gropius and Maxwell Fry
Client: Mr. Ben Levy

This house was planned for a site of limited size in a very busy street. To gain space for a large private garden, the house was placed with its length at right angles to the road. In 1936 it was inhabited by a family of five and several servants (Mrs. Levy was the well-known actress, Constance Cummings), but after the war it was enlarged by Jane Drew-Fry to accommodate two families.

The reaction of the English public in 1936 was best summed up in a report in the London Times, which also dwelt on the neighboring house built by Erich Mendelsohn and Serge Chermayeff: "In a sense these are the most advanced buildings in London, but the odd thing is that they not only tone in with the general character of the neighborhood, but seem to have a definite relationship to some old, possibly eighteenth century, houses on the same street. It is the nineteenth century that intrudes."

The Architectural Review expressed a similar view: "These two houses standing side by side on one side of the street, facing a row of typical and particularly charming Georgian houses . . . This situation enables the two houses to serve as a practical demonstration of the affinities between the Georgian and the modern house, the more so as the two are linked together by a continuous wall along the street frontage and have been designed with collaboration between the architects to ensure the lining up of roof lines and so on, recreating thereby some of the spirit and unity of the Georgian terrace type."

Another observation appeared in the January 1937 issue of Building: "In this street can clearly be seen how the modern movement takes up the tradition of English urban design at the point where it was laid down early in the 19th century—or, rather, submerged in the orgy of eclecticism that that century indulged in—the same studied proportion and relationship of parts that gave the Georgian its elegance, expressed with the same sense of rather impersonal restraint, in its modern equivalent."

Structural data: Brick walls, partly steel frame; balconies of reinforced concrete; roof; hollow-tile reinforced concrete, cork slabs with gravel surface; windows: sliding metal windows or metal casement windows; heating: panel heating in ceilings; external finish: stucco mixed with mica.

41
• **IMPINGTON VILLAGE COLLEGE, 1936**
Cambridgeshire, England
Architects: Walter Gropius and Maxwell Fry
Client: Henry Morris, Secretary of the Educational Committee of the County of Cambridge

The idea for this school was conceived by Henry Morris, who urged the provision of combined educational and recreational facilities, for adults as well as children, in small towns and rural areas, to help prevent the drift to the cities. The College is a secondary school for 240 children between 11 and 15 years of age. Linked to the one-story single-depth classroom block, with its large glass sliding doors giving free access to the open air, is a slightly curved building that contains rooms for adult courses as well as those for recreation and play. There is a hall seating 360, which serves as an auditorium for the children by day, and for adult assemblies and theatricals in the evenings.

Adjoining this is a dining room with kitchen attached, a common room, rooms for table tennis and billiards, a library, small lecture rooms, and a workshop for vocational education.

Nikolaus Pevsner, in his book on English buildings, describes the College as "one of the best buildings in England of its date, if not the best. Equally successful in its grouping and its setting among the trees of the Impington Hall Estate. The pattern for much to come (including most progressive schools built after the Second World War), in so far as at Impington the practical and visual advantages of modern forms in a loose, yet coherent arrangement had first been demonstrated." *

*Nikolaus Pevsner, *The Buildings of England: Cambridgeshire.* Penguin Books. London, 1954.

42

DORMITORY FOR CHRIST'S COLLEGE, 1936
Cambridge, England
Project
Architects: Walter Gropius and Maxwell Fry
Client: Christ's College

The proposal for a student dormitory at Christ's College presented an opportunity to extend the relationship between the city and the University —an unusual attempt at that time in England. The design recognized the street, providing an open meeting place, wide covered walks, parking, and an attractive triangular sculpture garden. The project was not realized because of the architects' refusal to comply with the University's proposal for a traditional façade on the side of the dormitory facing other University buildings.

43

• **GROPIUS RESIDENCE, 1937**
Lincoln, Massachusetts
Architects: Walter Gropius and Marcel Breuer
Client: Mrs. James Storrow

In 1937 Gropius gave a concrete example of his rejection of the label 'International Style.' He had stated: "I have always fought against this expression because I think the starting point is much more the idea of fulfilling regional conditions rather than obeying international precepts. There is only a superficial similarity because we have the same means of production all over the world." In the house that he built for himself and his family

at Lincoln, he made use of the traditional building materials of New England, both for the structure and for the exterior, but employed them in a way entirely new to that region. No component parts, from clapboard siding to doorknobs, were especially designed for the house. Everything could be obtained at the time from any building supply house in America; up to then, however, little had been created from these components except copies of period architecture.

The house stands on the crest of a low hill in the partly open, partly wooded countryside not far from Cambridge. The two-story building contains an entrance hall leading straight through to the screened porch, thus permitting cross ventilation. Dining and living room form a unit but can be divided by a curtain, while the study is separated from the dining area by a slanting glass-brick wall. This arrangement and the large windows make the rooms seem much larger than they actually are.

The roof-overhang protects the living and dining-room area against the hot summer sun, but is separated from the house wall by an opening that lets warm air escape. The west window is shielded by an outdoor aluminum venetian blind which deflects the sun's heat. From October to June the sun penetrates the whole living area. Small, built-in radiators along the big windows throw a curtain of warm air over the glass area to prevent drafts. The second floor contains two bedrooms and a combination bed and living room which is also accessible from the garden by an outdoor spiral staircase leading to a large terrace. The roof is slightly slanted toward the middle of the house so that rain and melting snow can be drained off through an interior pipe. After 30 years in the harsh climate of New England the house is still in excellent condition.

Structural data: light wood frame, sheathed with white-painted clapboard siding. Fireplace wall of gray-painted brick.

44

• **HAGERTY RESIDENCE, 1938**
Cohasset, Massachusetts
Architects: Walter Gropius and Marcel Breuer
Client: Mrs. Josephine Hagerty

This house was built for a rugged site overlooking the Atlantic Ocean and a rocky beach. It was equipped for year-round living.

Structural data: Combination of steel and

wood frame and rubble stone. All rubble stone was taken from the site. Concrete terrace under house. Wooden roof-deck covering. Large sliding glass door between living room and porch.

45

BLACK MOUNTAIN COLLEGE, 1939
near Asheville, North Carolina
Project
Architects: Walter Gropius and Marcel Breuer
Client: Black Mountain College

This project was to be the first major building complex planned for Black Mountain College. This small school, situated in the beautiful, wooded mountains of North Carolina, had attracted an unusually progressive faculty (among them some former Bauhaus members), all of whom were willing to make great financial sacrifices in order to preserve a totally independent stand in their teaching methods. To demonstrate their ideas effectively, the faculty decided that a new building was called for.

Situated on the curving shore of Lake Eden, the complex was to have included a student center with a dining room seating 230, rooms for music practice and an auditorium seating 144 (which could be expanded to seat 265), with adjoining stage workshops. A sloping, covered walk was to have led to a joint workshop and study building, which also was to house the infirmary. The adjacent building enclosed a large lobby area, with a roof terrace above and a garage underneath. At one end of the lobby was the main entrance to the complex, and at the other end there was a huge curved glass wall, which permitted an unobstructed view of the lake.

The outbreak of the Second World War interfered with these plans and they were never realized because of a shortage of funds.

46

• **CHAMBERLAIN RESIDENCE, 1939**
Sudbury, Massachusetts
Architects: Walter Gropius and Marcel Breuer
Client: H. Chamberlain

This house was built for an elderly couple who were devoted to nature and wildlife observation and wanted a very simple structure for casual living in the woods all year round. The free-standing fireplace is the outstanding feature of the interior, separating the living and dining areas.

Structural data: Wood frame, oiled redwood siding, steel casement windows, local stone substructure.

47

• FRANK RESIDENCE, 1939
Pittsburgh, Pennsylvania
Architects: Walter Gropius and Marcel Breuer
Client: Mr. Robert Frank

The house has a steel skeleton, with brick infill faced with light pink Indiana limestone. Window casements are steel, and roofing is copper. The house is completely air-conditioned, an unusual feature at the time. Particular attention was given to the landscaping of the site.

48

• ALUMINUM CITY TERRACE HOUSING, 1941
New Kensington, near Pittsburgh, Pennsylvania
Architects: Walter Gropius and Marcel Breuer
Client: Federal Works Agency (FWA),
Division of Defense Housing

Following the course taken by many major industrial areas unable to cope with the swelling numbers of workers during the Second World War, Pittsburgh launched a program of low-cost housing. Pittsburgh's program differed from the others, however, in that it recognized the value of quality in design. Thus when Gropius and Breuer were chosen as master planners and architects for "Aluminum City Terrace Housing," they were given considerable latitude in developing their solution, as well as encouragement in finding ways to improve low-cost housing standards. Initially, political and aesthetic controversies made the project a center of dispute, but after a year's residence, 89 percent of the working-class tenants—most of whom had never before been exposed to modern design—decided that they liked living in the new dwellings.

The Gropius-Breuer plan evolved out of a desire to preserve the natural quality of the hilly wooded site and to give each unit southern exposure and a view of open land. The 250 units were standardized, with only a few optional additions, and were arranged primarily in two-story rows with two or three bedrooms per unit. Adding variety to the development were 30 single-story,

one-bedroom units arranged in rows, and four semidetached houses perched on a hilltop that descended abruptly into a river valley. The latter houses had a cantilevered porch projecting from each end. The most startling design features were the ribbon windows on upper floors and the large lower floor windows, with slatted sun baffles to exclude the high summer sun and yet permit the lower winter sun to enter the living areas. Each unit had cross ventilation.

Floor plans of all three unit types were open—the living room giving onto the dining area and the kitchen separated only by a low partition. An indoor utility room in each unit provided storage and laundry space.

Structural data: Wood-frame construction; regularly spaced wood posts located at partitions between rooms support all vertical loads. Fronts of one- and two-story units have brick facing; all semidetached houses have treated cedar siding laid vertically.

49

PACKAGED HOUSE SYSTEM, 1942/52
Designed and patented by Walter Gropius and
Konrad Wachsmann
Client: General Panel Corporation

The basic idea of this system was similar to the Copper House of Hirsch-Kupfer (see No. 35) but the wall panels were much lighter and easier to handle. The system consisted of prefabricated elements based on the same module and thus interchangeable. A complex, three-dimensional interlocking metal joint or 'wedge connector' allowed a variety of combinations. The wood panels could be assembled vertically or horizontally to form walls, floor, ceiling, or roof. This method made possible the production of easily transportable and easily assembled unit parts instead of stereotyped completely standardized houses.

Mass production of the Packaged House System was started in California in 1949 and proved a success. Unfortunately it had to be discontinued in 1952, not because of technical difficulties, but because of limitations in financing methods, which were still based entirely on conventional construction time schedules. It was not feasible for a manufacturer of prefabricated houses to wait 6 to 8 months until federal financing was processed.

50

HOWLETT RESIDENCE, 1948
Belmont, Massachusetts
Architect: The Architects Collaborative (TAC)*
Principals-in-charge: Walter Gropius, Ben Thompson
Client: Mr. Clarence Howlett

This is a three-level dwelling with a large open center containing living room, dining room, playroom, and stairs. Each level opens to a separate terrain with a different character. Although split levels may give a house complexity, an attempt was made in this design to attain simplicity and homogeneity. The open plan gives a sense of spaciousness, and the split level, dividing living and sleeping areas, assures privacy where needed. The upper level consists of bedrooms, bath, and storage.

To the nearby street the house presents a discreet cypress-wood front with a low silhouette to blend with a conventional neighborhood. On the side away from the street the large open center of the house has a glass wall facing south to tree-covered rolling ground.

Structural data: Light wood frame with lally-columns, cypress sheathing.

*Hereafter the abbreviation "TAC" is used for the firm name "The Architects Collaborative."

51

• HARVARD GRADUATE CENTER, 1949
Cambridge, Massachusetts
Architect: TAC
Principals-in-charge: Walter Gropius, Norman C. Fletcher, Louis A. McMillen, Ben Thompson
Client: Harvard University

This group of dormitories for 575 students, and the commons building with lounges and dining rooms serving 3000 students in shifts, constituted TAC's first commission of a magnitude greater than private homes. The spatial pattern of the Harvard campus, a consistent sequence of courtyards of varying sizes and shapes, was maintained by the architects on the theory that well-shaped open spaces between buildings are as important as the form of the buildings themselves. Emphasis was laid on creating an illusion of motion from one open space to another. Because of a very stringent budget the dormitories are identical, but their oblique orientation to the commons building, plus the interlocking arrangement of paths and open spaces, provides the visitor with constant changes in view.

The 223 single and 176 double rooms in the dormitories were assigned to students in different fields, thereby counteracting professional isolation. The dining rooms and lounges, being open to all students, provide a place for getting together and exchanging ideas.

In front of the slightly curved commons building, a large sunken plot of lawn can be turned in winter into a brightly illuminated skating rink, visible through the large glass façades of the lounges and dining rooms. The three dining rooms on the second floor are reached from the concourse by a free-standing concrete ramp which leads to the food service area. Paintings by Joan Miró and Herbert Bayer and relief sculptures by Hans Arp accentuate the rooms. The concourse is separated from the lounge and music room by a brick relief designed by Josef Albers. In front of the commons building stands a stainless steel sculpture by Richard Lippold.

Structural data: The dormitories are constructed of white, reinforced concrete frames with buff brick walls; the commons building has a steel frame faced with limestone or sky-blue glazed bricks.

52

BACK BAY CENTER DEVELOPMENT, 1953
Boston, Massachusetts
Project
Architects: Boston Center Architects (TAC in collaboration with Pietro Belluschi, Carl Koch, Walter Bogner, Hugh Stubbins)
TAC Principals-in-charge: Walter Gropius, Norman C. Fletcher
Client: Stevens Development Corp., Cleveland

This project received the First Design Award in the *Progressive Architecture* design awards program in 1954. It was to have included a shopping center, department store, supermarket, four office buildings, a combination hotel and motel, an exhibition building, convention hall and parking space for 6000 cars below the shopping and office level.

The 30 acre site was situated in the heart of Boston on an abandoned railroad yard. Within the Center people would have been able to participate in practically all phases of modern living without being disturbed by automobile traffic. For ease of access, two subway lines were planned, terminating in a station from which there would be direct escalator connection with the Center; the latter could also have been reached on foot from the downtown areas.

The project was never realized because of the impossibility of obtaining the necessary tax relief during the construction period.

53

• **INTERBAU APARTMENT BLOCK, 1956**
Berlin, Germany
Architect: TAC
Principals-in-charge: Walter Gropius, Norman C. Fletcher, H. Morse Payne
Contact Architect: Wils Ebert, Berlin
Client: The City of Berlin and Aktiengesellschaft für den Aufbau des Hansaviertels

This nine-story apartment building is part of a development designed by an international group of architects on a site in the center of Berlin that was almost totally destroyed by bombing—the Hansaviertel. It contains 64 three-bedroom units for middle-income families, plus two larger pent-house apartments. Intentionally, the plan of the apartments is not an open one, but each room is separately accessible from a hall. Since the apartments are rented by families of varying sizes and habits, this type of layout is more flexible than an open plan, at the same time giving greater privacy to individuals of any age. In some cases the living room and the adjacent bedroom are separated only by a curtain or a folding door instead of a wall, thereby allowing a large area for social gatherings and providing cross ventilation. Part of the ground floor can be used as a playroom for children.

Structural data: Reinforced concrete skeleton with wall fillings of blocks made of bomb rubble. Three different textures of white enliven the façade —smooth white stucco against rough white stucco, and white enameled balcony enclosures of steel panels combined with sky-blue soffits under the balconies.

54

• **UNITED STATES EMBASSY, 1956/61**
Athens, Greece
Architect: TAC
Principals-in-charge: Walter Gropius, H. Morse Payne
Contact Architect: Perikles Sakellarios, Athens
Client: US State Department, Office of Foreign Building Operations

The design of the US Embassy, situated one mile from the Parthenon at the foot of Mt. Lykabettos, derives from the serene strength of ancient Greek architecture and yet is expressed through modern structural techniques. The three-story building consists of a square around a landscaped interior plaza, which is open on one side to the landscaped slope bordering on one of Athens' big avenues leading to the city center.

Structural data: The structure is of reinforced concrete sheathed with white Pentelic marble. The two upper floors are hung from large concrete girders, each carried by a pair of 30 ft. columns placed peripherally around the four exterior elevations and those of the interior plaza. Thus the principal mass of the building appears to hover over the site. This main structure supports a 20 ft. overhanging "umbrella" roof which shields the two upper floors from the intense radiance of the Greek sky. Open slots allow hot air to escape. The roof itself is double layered to protect the upper-most floor from the sun's heat. Aluminum grills between the girders ventilate the roof space. A light-blue ceramic wall protects the ground floor from the sun. Gray glare-reducing glass is used for the fenestration. Flexibility of space for possible changes has been achieved through an integrated modular system of utilities.

55

"THE UNIVERSAL SCHOOL," 1957
Prototype project
Architect: TAC
Principals-in-charge: Walter Gropius, Norman C. Fletcher
Client: *Collier's Magazine,* Crowell-Collier Publishing Company, New York

Designed as a prototype for a highly flexible elementary school from kindergarten through sixth grade, the school made use of a cluster system that is adaptable to changing site and climatic conditions; it is also suitable for different building materials for the structural skeleton (wood, steel or concrete) and for the filler panels. By adding extra units, the school may be enlarged in any direction without disturbing existing buildings.

In essence, the school is a complex of four

classroom units, strung together in any direction as determined by the contours of the site, the orientation to the sun, and the prevailing wind. The central unit between four classrooms serves as a common room for the cluster. Each unit has a plexiglas dome in addition to the outside wall windows. Adjacent to each classroom there is a sheltered open play area, which may also be used as an outdoor classroom or a garden laboratory. Wardrobe and storage cabinets can be shifted at will. A multipurpose room, administration offices, auditorium and gymnasium may be added according to the requirements of the individual school program.

Structural data: The unit is a one-story class-room pavilion with four columns (spot foundations) and four beams, with the roof cantilevered on all sides to the width of each corridor. The size of the classroom may be varied by putting the panel walls between columns, under the eaves, or in both places. The space under the roof overhang may also serve as a connecting corridor, either open or glassed in.

56

• **THE UNIVERSITY OF BAGHDAD, 1957**
Baghdad, Iraq
Architect: TAC
Principals-in-charge: Walter Gropius, Louis A. McMillen, H. Morse Payne, Richard Brooker, Peter W. Morton, Robert McMillan
Contact Architect: Hisham A. Munir & Associates, Baghdad
Client: Government of the Republic of Iraq, Ministry of Works and Housing

Walter Gropius gives the following description of this task: "It is unusual in an architect's career that he is ever given the opportunity to design a large complex of buildings on a virgin site where he is able to establish the relationships between buildings and all the elements of the site and then proceed to prepare the working drawings for the whole, controlling the design of every detail. The University of Baghdad was just such an oppor-tunity. It began as an unprogrammed idea. Two typewritten pages were all we received from the client by way of guidance. From this we designed the entire organizational, educational, and physical plant of a complete university for 12,000 students."

The project consists of 273 buildings, ranging in size from a 5000-seat auditorium to individual houses for the faculty. The University may in fact be called a small town, designed to house and educate a large group of students. It will offer courses in three major fields: engineering, science and the humanities. The academic buildings are loosely arranged around an open square the size of the Piazza di San Marco in Venice. Divided into three general instruction areas planned for flexible use of space, rather than into distinct building groups, each division and the colleges within it is marked by functionally-related permanent adminis-trative areas. Apart from the obvious economic advantages gained from avoiding the duplication of facilities, the proximity and interchangeability of the three main divisions provide opportunities for the exchange of ideas by students working in the various areas of specialization, thereby fostering a breadth of intellectual development beyond the student's major field of study. To this end, small student lounges are dispersed throughout the academic area to bring students into daily informal contact.

The architectural character of the buildings has been determined by the peculiar climatic conditions: the excessive sun heat and the intense luminosity. A system of horizontal and vertical sun baffles, as protection against direct sun rays and carefully devised for each orientation, creates interpenetrating planes which result in a lively play of sunlight on the façades.

The site plan shows a composition of courts that vary in size and design. The buildings are close together in order to gain the maximum shade and to cut down circulation distances between the various parts of the large complex. Water, an important symbol in Arab life, is used extensively in fountains and canals. The whole site is irrigated by pumping water from the main circular canal surrounding the academic buildings in the center. This canal is filled from the Tigris River, which bounds the site on three sides.

Although the country has seen a good deal of political unrest since the University's formative stages and the project has consequently been delayed, construction has been underway since 1962, thanks to the perseverance of the Iraqi Government.

Structural data: The structure of the buildings is of reinforced concrete using local cement, sand and aggregate. Variety in the appearance of surfaces of structural elements and on prefab-ricated filler panels is achieved by different treatments such as exposed imprint of form work, bush hammering or sandblasting, and by the use of white or gray cement. A sequence of brightly colored wall-surfaces supplies lively accents to the campus, as well as providing orientation. Many of the buildings are fully air-conditioned and all are equipped with heating facilities.

57

• **PAN AMERICAN WORLD AIRWAYS BUILDING, 1958/63**
New York, NY
Architect: Emery Roth and Sons
Consulting Architects: Walter Gropius and Pietro Belluschi
Client: Grand Central Building, Inc., New York

The Pan Am Building, fifty-nine stories high and containing 2,350,000 square feet of office space for about 25,000 people, is located at the inter-section of Park Avenue and 44th Street above the subterranean part of Grand Central Terminal, the center for all rail and subway transportation in New York.

At the outset the consulting architects were asked to work on the basis of an earlier proposal for a building of much larger size which, at that time, was well within the building laws. Before accepting the commission, however, they persuaded Mr. Erwin S. Wolfson, president of Grand Central Building, Inc., to scale the building down to 2,500,000 square feet, which they felt was an urbanistically more acceptable solution.

The design in its final form was developed by Walter Gropius and Pietro Belluschi in association with Emery Roth & Sons. The initial proposal was for a tower on top of a six-story base building enclosing a courtyard, to give the entire complex a sense of lightness. This scheme proved financially untenable, since it is the base building, with its enormous horizontal expanse, that brings in the highest rents. The courtyard was therefore given over to rental space and the height of the base building increased to nine stories. Eighty percent of the offices were rented out prior to construction, largely to the Pan American World Airways Company.

The eight-faceted tower, set off from its base by two transitional levels, catches the light with different intensities, thereby lending a sculptural quality to the building. To relieve the straight ascent there are two recessed sections girdling the building. The greater width of the tower at midpoint results logically from the placement of the elevators in the center, while its unusual prismatic shape places it in strong contrast to the rectangular shapes of the other skyscrapers in the vicinity.

Since the building straddles Park Avenue, general pedestrian traffic is led straight through the two-story lobby by a concourse, while automotive traffic runs along its two sides on ramps in order to avoid bottlenecks. The building is recessed at street level to form shopping arcades. Offices command splendid views across the entire width of Manhattan, from the Hudson to the East River, and up and down Park Avenue.

In addition to the three main entrances, provision has been made for four private entrance and lobby areas, each with its own service and elevator core. Garage space was intentionally kept limited, since the Grand Central Terminal handles the bulk of commuters and since automotive traffic in the inner city was not to be encouraged.

The garages are accessible from both the streets and the ramps. A rooftop heliport is equipped to provide five-minute service to and from the New York airports. Three restaurants on the ground floor have dining facilities for 6000 persons, while a private dining room is located on the 56th floor. In addition there is a mobile canteen service throughout the building.

From the beginning, Gropius intended that the contributions of artists should be an integral part of the design: a wire sculpture by Richard Lippold stretches from floor to ceiling of the two-story lobby, and a laminated plastic mural by Josef Albers and a metal screen by Gyorgy Kepes are located in the main lobby.

In planning such an urban complex the aim was to provide short horizontal distances that promote pedestrian rather than vehicular traffic in the inner city. It has been proved that a concentration of high building masses facilitates business by replacing horizontal with vertical traffic (here by 64 elevators and 18 escalators). Since the building is visited daily by a quarter of a million people, the reduction of street traffic is of great importance.

In the subsequent controversies over the building, Gropius took the position that the accumulation of high-rise buildings on Park Avenue called for a monumental focus astride the Avenue, corresponding in height and scale to the changed townscape around it and giving the endless row of buildings a point of reference. Years of observation

since have shown that no traffic jams occurred, and that in fact the area has become decongested in spite of the added volume of the building.

Structural data: The skeleton of structural steel, the exterior walls of precast concrete elements studded with white quartz. The floors are prefabricated steel panels, and the window frames are of dark anodized aluminum, pivoted vertically so that the windows can be cleaned from inside. Venetian blinds give protection against sunlight. 10,000 main telephones were installed. The Pan Am Building was erected without interrupting the operation of railway and subway service.

58
• GROPIUSSTADT, 1959/71
Berlin-Buckow-Rudow, Germany
Architect: TAC
Principals-in-charge: Walter Gropius,
Alex Cvijanovic
Contact Architects: Wils Ebert, Hans Bandel, and
Heinz Viehrig, Berlin
Client: The City of Berlin

A new township has been added to West Berlin in the southern part of the district of Neukoelln, the last portion of an area of land that stretches from the 'Horseshoe Housing Development' (Hufeisensiedlung) built between 1925 and 1931, to the border of East Berlin. The 650-acre site will provide 17,000 dwelling units, as well as new schools, nurseries, recreation areas, parks and shopping centers to serve 50,000 people in the low-to-moderate income group. All parts of the development will be connected by pedestrian walkways. The basic concept was to create a dense and self-sufficient urban community, using the most advanced prefabrication techniques and construction systems available.

TAC developed the urban design concept in 1959. Anticipating current concern with environmental issues, the master plan restricted automobiles and service vehicles to roads on the perimeter. To reduce pollution, a smokeless power plant provides heat and hot water for the whole community. A green belt traverses the entire site. The tree-lined pedestrian mall running from east to west not only links the building groups to each other, but also to adjoining neighborhoods, particularly to the schools, churches and shopping centers. The community is served by a subway line to downtown West Berlin, a half-hour trip.

After the plan was set up, a number of non-profit building organizations, subsidized by the Federal Government and the City of Berlin, were commissioned with the execution of different sections of the project. Architects were chosen through local competitions, under the combined guidance of Walter Gropius and the various organizations.

TAC designed three groups of apartment buildings (1964) for 1100 units, distributed in blocks: low-rise, high-rise semicircular and low-rise plus a 30-story tower. TAC was also commissioned to design an experimental school to serve all children between the ages of five and eighteen living within a one-mile radius, and a children's day-care center.

The narrow strip of forest land, with its bird sanctuary, extending in from the green belt, provides a backdrop for the buildings. By repetition of certain design elements in all of the buildings, unity was maintained despite the different developers.

A building-code restriction requiring that each major room receive a minimum of two hours of sunlight during 270 days of the year was the major criterion for the orientation of the buildings. Rather than specializing the buildings by apartment types, all buildings contain a mixture of apartment sizes. Since each apartment is comparatively small, great attention was paid to circulation patterns, so that active daytime areas would be separated from the quieter nighttime ones.

Structural data: Each of the three developers used different industrialized building systems for their projects. Gehag's six nine-story blocks are built with masonry bearing walls with cast-in-place concrete slabs. Factory precast exterior wall panels are used both as infill and as cladding for the structural frame. Hilfswerk's sixteen-story building is built with a precast structural panel building system. Ideal's thirty-story tower was built with concrete slab and wall elements and cement-asbestos infill panels.

59
• JOHN F. KENNEDY FEDERAL BUILDING, 1961/66
Boston, Massachusetts
Architects: TAC in association with Samuel
Glaser & Associates
TAC principals-in-charge: Walter Gropius,
Norman C. Fletcher
Client: US General Services Administration

The John F. Kennedy Federal Building is part of the new Government Center which is grouped around the new Boston City Hall. An area of 60 acres was provided for the Center; of these 16 acres represented malls and squares extending through the entire renewal area and beyond. The main plaza stretches between the City Hall, the Kennedy Building and abutting streets on sloping, terraced ground with radially patterned brick paving and a sunken fountain. The master plan was designed by I. M. Pei, who succeeded in uniting new and old buildings into a beautiful cityscape.

The Kennedy Building consists of a 26-story tower and a 4-story building. The high-rise tower is split into two halves with elevator stacks in between, achieving thereby a slender appearance and ensuring direct daylight for almost all of the offices. A large mural, ''New England Elegy,'' by Robert Motherwell, is placed over the entrance to the glass-enclosed corridor linking the low building to the tower. The spaciousness of the plaza is emphasized by the 16-foot bronze ''Thermopylae'' by Dimitri Hadzi.

The gross area of the building is about 1,000,000 square feet, and the net usable area is approximately 672,000 square feet on a site of 4½ acres.

Structural data: The office spaces are made flexible by modular planning based on a 4'10" square grid carried throughout the exterior and the interior, coordinating ceilings, lighting, heating, air-conditioning, partitions, and underfloor cable systems. Pivoted anodized aluminum windows allow cleaning from the interior. The steel frame tower has 14 elevators, the reinforced concrete low building five elevators and two escalators.

60

• COMBINED SCHOOL & DAY CARE CENTER,
1962/68
Gropiusstadt, Berlin, Germany
Architect: TAC
Principals-in-charge: Walter Gropius,
Alex Cvijanovic
Contact Architect: Wils Ebert, Berlin
Client: The Berlin Senate

This school complex provides educational facilities for 1500 children between the ages of two and eighteen living within a one-mile radius in the new urban community called Gropiusstadt. Gropius persuaded the school board to put into action German proposals for a new school program, radically different from the traditional system. The goal of this 'Comprehensive School' is to introduce more individualization and differentiation into the educational system; the architects' design was based on the requirements resulting from this new approach.

The school is divided into kindergarten, elementary and high school. The plan calls for the following: 3 two-story elementary schools, 2 three-story high schools, 1 three-story science building with laboratory classrooms, 1 workshop building, 1 large sports hall, 1 smaller hall for gymnastics and remedial exercises, 1 kindergarten, and 1 day care center for children between two and fourteen years of age.

The problem of direct access into the classrooms from the outside, of direct attachment of classrooms to the multipurpose rooms, and of cross ventilation for each classroom were solved by grouping six-sided classrooms around a central space. The eight school buildings connect by walkways that are glass enclosed on one side.

Each of the three elementary school pavilions contains two groups of three classrooms, with access to the two-story multipurpose room. Connected with this central area are a teachers' room, study rooms, cafeteria, reading balcony and cloakrooms.

The high school pavilions, each three stories high, provide five classrooms in each story, clustered around a multipurpose room.

The science building houses laboratories, a library, model kitchens, music and administration rooms.

The kindergarten, located in one wing of the Day Care Center, belongs to the general educational system of the Comprehensive School. The interiors are furnished with child-size playhouses for the two- to five-year-olds. The Day Care Center, for children of working mothers, includes two covered outdoor play spaces, one of which can be used as an outdoor theater.

Structural data: Reinforced concrete poured in place. The exposed structural parts are sandblasted; all other surfaces are covered with smooth, precast concrete panels with a special surface aggregate or with surface ribbing. Windows are double glazed.

The colored ceramic mural on the exterior, and all interior color specifications for the buildings are by Lou Scheper-Berkenkamp.

61

• BAUHAUS ARCHIVE, 1964
Berlin, Germany
Architect: TAC
Principals-in-charge: Walter Gropius,
Alex Cvijanovic
Client: The City of Berlin

First conceived for a site on the Mathildenhöhe in Darmstadt, the original location of the Bauhaus Archive, the building will now be erected in Berlin for occupancy in 1973. The design for the Bauhaus Archive is so planned that all preserved documents which relate to the history and prehistory of the Bauhaus, and a great number of objects, artifacts and works of art which were produced in the Bauhaus, can be made available for study. Furthermore, the Bauhaus Archive will continue its research into the relationship between art and technology.

The building will contain a public library with lecture hall, a museum, exhibition rooms, administrative and study rooms and a cafeteria. Public rooms are so situated that they can be used after normal working hours with only a minimal staff present.

Various kinds of vaulted skylights and adaptable lighting installations in coffered ceilings illuminate the interior. Natural light is admitted as much as possible, since the architects hold that the visitor, whether viewing works of art or pursuing his studies, needs to refresh and relax his eyes and mind by a glimpse of the outside world. Moreover, they preferred the dynamic of the natural light in its effect on paintings and sculpture: ''Natural light . . . is dynamic, is alive, as it changes continuously. The 'fleeting occurrence' caused by the change of light is 'just what we desire'.''*

*Walter Gropius, *Apollo in the Democracy*. McGraw Hill Publishing Company. New York, 1968.

62

PLACE SAINT-CYRILLE, 1964
Quebec, Canada
Project
Architect: TAC
Principal-in-charge: Walter Gropius
Client: Mondey Corporation, Montreal

This plan for a new business center opposite Quebec's Houses of Parliament was to have included a hotel with 400 rooms and convention facilities, a department store, two high-rise office buildings, an apartment house with 100 units, a movie theater and an underground parking lot for 1000 cars. Pedestrian arcades and shops were to line the widened Boulevard Saint-Cyrille and lead past the two office buildings to the opposite side of the complex.

This project could not be carried out because the Prime Minister ruled against the development of the site since it might conflict with future expansion of the Parliament buildings.

Structural data: Reinforced concrete with an exterior façade of prefabricated concrete slabs.

63

• CHINA FACTORY "ROSENTHAL AM ROTBUHL" 1965/66
Selb, Germany
Architect: TAC
Principals-in-charge: Walter Gropius,
Alex Cvijanovic
Client: Rosenthal A.G., Selb

This industrial complex is composed of a large single-story factory (2,000,000 sq. ft.), an administration building, a garage, a raw-material silo, a waste silo, and a two-story social center. Set in the open, rolling countryside, it is entered through a single canopied main entrance gate with porter's lodge; this opens onto a large brick-paved courtyard around which the various buildings are grouped. Deep roof overhangs, exterior support columns and painted emergency exits jutting from the sides of the buildings articulate the façades. The exterior of the lower floors and the supporting walls have a vertically grooved surface.

In addition to the planning of an efficient production process, special emphasis was put on social and psychological considerations. In artificially lighted working spaces, narrow windows reaching to the ceiling serve to refresh the eye. The aisles between the machines terminate in wall areas finished with brightly colored ceramic tiles, providing visual orientation. At the intersection of all main communication paths there is a greenhouse for tropical plants and birds, a pleasing contrast to the monotony of the machine shops. The information center, located between the administration and production areas, dispenses local and international news as well as reports on production; it also serves as a place for product exhibitions. It acts as

a center for stimulation and relaxation, through which all employees have to pass.

The highest structure is the three-story social center, where employees meet for recreational, sporting and educational activities. It contains a dining and entertainment hall for 300 to 400 people, a kitchen and auxiliary facilities.

Structural data: Complete flexibility has been achieved by prefabrication of all parts, structural and nonstructural, in order that changes can be made without interfering with production. Outside walls as well as T-shaped columns, connecting beams, supporting purlins, concrete planks, and ventilating skylights can be disassembled and re-erected. The main structural element is the 'hammerhead' column, especially developed for this project. This construction method requires a horizontal roof without pitch. The grid is a bay system of 33 ft. x 33 ft., allowing efficient use of space for all assembly lines, including transport routes and aisles.

64

SELB TOWN PLAN, 196?
Selb, Germany
Planner: TAC
Principals-in-charge: Walter Gropius,
Alex Cvijanovic
Client: The Town of Selb

Selb is a town of 20,000 inhabitants with major access routes from Bayreuth and Nuremberg. It is surrounded by forest and hilly farmland. After having been totally destroyed by fire during the last century, the town gradually became the center of the ceramics industry. It lacks a true focal point or center, it is plagued by traffic congestion and lack of parking areas, industrial railway sidings cross major streets, the streams are polluted, and new residential subdivisions bear no relationship to the existing town or to each other. The town is therefore considered drab and not particularly desirable to live in, and the lack of an adequate labor supply has discouraged the expansion of industry.

Since the plight of this town is becoming a more and more familiar pattern everywhere, Gropius, together with Alex Cvijanovic, was willing to accept a commission to produce a development plan for the town's future. The town fathers had previously commissioned Professor Leibbrand, a consulting traffic engineer, to draw up a comprehensive traffic plan. Together with him, Gropius,

Alex Cvijanovic and others worked as a team to integrate traffic planning with the town plan.

Gropius believed that the solution for the future does not necessarily call for new towns but rather for the extension of existing ones in a planned and continuous process. He felt that the town as a living organism should be planned for continuity of change and that certain desirable qualities of the past and present should be restored and carried into the future. Among these were the safety and convenience of the pedestrian. His proposal therefore called for winning back the town center for the pedestrian by clearing it of all vehicular traffic, while providing parking nearby.

Other important objectives included the general revitalization of the core by creating an area devoted to cultural events, evening entertainment, restaurant service, shops, and so on.

The solution to the traffic problems is seen in providing a major belt highway to connect the outlying sectors of the town, superimposed on a system of three major arteries that cross near the center of town, forming a rough triangle to contain the pedestrian area. Short service roads lead from this triangle to nearby parking facilities and provide automotive access to public and commercial buildings within the core.

Selb lies at the confluence of a number of valleys which send a system of green fingers into the town. These will become locations for sports facilities, kindergartens, schools, playgrounds, and so on. Housing areas will be developed on hillsides bordering the new greenways. Single-family houses are proposed for the bottom of the slope, three-story walk-ups in the middle and high-rise apartment blocks (about nine stories) at the top near the traffic arteries.

Three intermediate stages of development, geared to population growth, were proposed so that various projects would be undertaken in a logical sequence.

65

• THOMAS GLASS FACTORY, 1968
Amberg, Germany
Architect: TAC
Principals-in-charge: Walter Gropius,
Alex Cvijanovic
Client: Rosenthal A.G., Amberg

The focal point of this glass factory is a 63 ft. 9 in. high manufacturing "nave," triangular in section, located slightly below eye level as seen from the access road. This section results in the roof rather than the exterior walls forming the façade of the factory. Although the design is based on the functional requirements of the manufacturing process, the main interior also forms an unusual architectural space.

The complex consists of four buildings: the central manufacturing space containing furnaces, a casting area, raw material silos and processing areas; two laterally extending low buildings for offices, laboratories, workshops, storage, etc.; a low building at the front of the central plant for medical services, washrooms and a recreation room for employees.

The central space is connected to the adjacent low buildings by glass-enclosed passages. This arrangement forms a series of small landscaped courtyards, which can be seen and enjoyed from the interior and visited during rest periods.

The glass furnaces in the main hall radiate enormous quantities of heat in spite of their ample insulation and the glass is processed in open space at temperatures from 1292° to 2372°F. Quick and efficient heat extraction is provided without mechanical air-conditioning. The entire walls of the main hall can be opened or closed by wide pivoted doors, so that if necessary the whole length of the building can be open at ground level. The hot air streams through a ventilation slot along the ridge of the roof, pulling in fresh air from ground level. The aerodynamically designed roof shape facilitates this process.

Structural data: The building is based on a 30 ft. x 30 ft. module. The central nave has a 65-foot span. The distance between roof girders is 30 feet. Between the girders prestressed concrete slats are set in an overlapping waterproof pattern. No other roof covering is needed. The jalousied slats also ensure very good lighting of the interior while excluding direct sunlight. The main hall is designed so that any number of structural bays may be added for expansion.

66
• CHINA TEA SET "TAC 1," 1968
• CHINA COFFEE SET "TAC 2," 1968
Designer: TAC
Principals-in-charge: Walter Gropius,
Louis A. McMillen
Client: Rosenthal A.G., Selb

The characteristic shape of the tea set is based on the wide form of the traditional teacup, but the latter's proportions are reversed for the pot, the creamer and the sugar bowl. In pouring, the lid is automatically secured by the thumb when the handle of the teapot is grasped.

The open spout and the open handle of the coffee pot make the design unusual. It was found that a spout formed as an open groove pours better and cleans more easily than the traditional spout.

Basic functional forms, rather than those dictated by fashion, were what the designers had in mind.

The tea set is internationally available.

67
• TOWER EAST OFFICE COMPLEX, 1968
Shaker Heights, Cleveland, Ohio
Architect: TAC
Principal-in-charge: Walter Gropius
Client: Central Cadillac Company, Cleveland

This office complex represents the solution to the problem of designing a major building to be integrated with its surroundings and solving the urban problems associated with the site. The site selected was a major traffic junction of seven streets. The client concurred with the architects' opinion that "a strong landmark providing visual orientation" was needed, though the zoning law did not permit high-rise buildings. Only after the client obtained a variance could the project be realized. The final solution is carried out in two phases. Phase I is a completed twelve-story high-rise office building with a total of 207,000 square feet, accompanied by an adjacent six-story garage for 600 cars and 60 surface parking places. Phase II will consist of a four-story office building with an underground concourse connecting the high-rise building to the parking garage. Two stories will be added to the garage, for an ultimate capacity of 800 cars.

The building of Phase I is set on a sloping site, allowing two levels for automobile traffic and general commercial space. The first two stories contain a restaurant seating 450 with an adjoining outdoor sculpture terrace, a drive-in bank, four specialty shops with mezzanines, and the main two-story lobby. Each of the ten upper stories has a rental area of approximately 14,000 square feet. The principal tenant, occupying 60,000 square feet of office space, also commissioned the architects

to design interiors and to supervise the acquisition of more than thirty contemporary works of art.

Structural data: The structural frame is reinforced concrete with a one-way joist system using 30 inch wide metal pan forms. Only two interior columns stand in the rentable area of each floor; otherwise floors are supported from the building core to perimeter columns. The exposed structural gray concrete is sandblasted, with reveals separating the concrete pours. White precast exterior panels are visually set off from the gray structural concrete. An integral part of the precast panel, slanted concrete shades reduce sun glare. Window glass is a heat-absorbent solar gray, framed by deep aluminum sashes with a dark bronze finish. Air-conditioning is supplied through special recessed light fixtures and is on a single-duct variable volume system.

68
• GERMAN AMBASSADOR'S RESIDENCE, 1968
Buenos Aires, Argentina
Project
Architect: TAC
Principals-in-charge: Walter Gropius,
Alex Cvijanovic
Contact Architect: Amancio Williams,
Buenos Aires
Client: The Federal Republic of Germany

The design for this project capitalizes on the unusual site provided for the client by the City of Buenos Aires—a large tree-covered public park in the center of the city. It was of primary importance to the city fathers that the pedestrian's view be unobstructed by the new building. Thus the design calls for lowering the first floor of the structure and raising the second level approximately 20 feet to treetop level. The surrounding trees would be retained as an integral part of the design and landscaping; in particular, the roof of the lower section of the building, which is to be entirely covered with greenery, would create a sense of continuity with the surrounding park grounds.

The residence consists of two main functional areas. The reception rooms, which occupy the more public-oriented first level, include a large hall, music salon, library and dining room, all built around a sunken covered courtyard. The living quarters of the Ambassador and his family on the second level also include an inner open court.

Structural data: Concrete frame and exterior.

Selected Bibliography

Works by Walter Gropius

Staatliches Bauhaus in Weimar, 1919/23
    Bauhaus Verlag, Weimar-München, 1923
Internationale Architektur
    Bauhausbücher Bd. 1, Albert Langen.
    München, 1925
Bauhausbauten Dessau
    Bauhausbücher Bd. 12, Albert Langen,
    München, 1930
The New Architecture and the Bauhaus
    Faber and Faber Ltd., London, 1935, 1936,
    1937, 1955, 1965 paperback
    Massachusetts Institute of Technology Press,
    Cambridge, 1965 paperback
    Florian Kupferberg Verlag, Mainz, 1964
    (German edition)
    Editorial Lumen, Barcelona, 1966 paperback
    La Connaissance S.A., Bruxelles, 1966
    paperback
Bauhaus 1919–1928 by Walter and Ise Gropius
    and Herbert Bayer
    The Museum of Modern Art, New York, 1938
    Charles T. Branford Company, Boston, 1952
    Verlag Gerd Hatje, Stuttgart, 1955
Rebuilding Our Communities
    Paul Theobald, Chicago, 1946
Scope of Total Architecture
    Harper and Brothers, New York, 1955
    George Allen & Unwin, London, 1956
    Collier Books, New York, 1962 paperback
    Architektur' Wege zu einer optischen Kultur
    Fischer Bücherei, Frankfurt-Hamburg, 1956
    Alcances de la arquitectura integral
    Ediciones La Isla, Buenos Aires, 1956
    Scope of Total Architecture (in Japanese)
    Charles E. Tuttle Company, Tokyo, 1958

Architettura integrata
    Arnoldo Mondadori, Milan, 1959
Sinteza u architekturi
    Zagreb, Yugoslavia, 1961
Architettura integrata
    Il Saggiatore, Milan, 1963 paperback
Arquitectura y Planeamiento
    Ediciones Infinito, Buenos Aires, 1958
The Architects Collaborative, Inc.
    Arthur Niggli, Teufen, Switzerland, 1966
    (English-German edition)
    Gustav Gili, Barcelona, Spain, 1972
    (English-Spanish edition)
Apollo in der Demokratie
    Florian Kupferberg Verlag, Mainz, 1967
    Apolo en la Democracia
    Monte Avila Editores, C.A., Caracas, 1968
    *Apollo in the Democracy: The Cultural
    Obligation of the Architect*
    McGraw-Hill Book Company, New York, 1968
    *Apolon dans la democratie et La nouvelle
    architecture et le Bauhaus*
    La Connaissance S.A., Bruxelles, 1969
    paperback

Works about Walter Gropius

    Giulio Carlo Argan:
Gropius e la Bauhaus, Giulio Einaudi, Turin, 1951
German edition: Rowohlt Taschenbuch Verlag, 1962
Spanish edition: Editorial Nueva Vision, Buenos
Aires, 1957
    Sigfried Giedion:
Walter Gropius, G. Crès & Cie., Paris, 1931
Walter Gropius, Work and Teamwork, Reinhold
Publishing Co., New York, 1954
Walter Gropius, Mensch und Werk, Gerd Hatje

Verlag, Stuttgart, 1954
Walter Gropius, L'Homme et L'Oeuvre, Editions
A. Morancé, Paris, 1954
Walter Gropius, L'Uomo e l'Opera, Edizione di
Communita, Milan, 1954
    Chikatada Kurata, Y. Nosu & M. Koyama:
Walter Gropius, Bizyutu-Syuppan-Sya Ltd.,
Tokyo, 1954
    International House of Japan:
Gropius in Japan, Tokyo, 1965
    Gilbert Herbert:
The Synthetic Vision of Walter Gropius,
Witwatersrand University Press, Johannesburg,
1959
    James Marston Fitch:
Walter Gropius, George Braziller, New York, 1960
German edition: Otto Mayer Verlag, Ravensburg
Italian edition: Il Saggiatore, Milan
    Helmut Weber:
Walter Gropius und das Faguswerk, Callwey
Verlag, 1961
    Hans M. Wingler:
Bauhaus Weimar-Dessau-Berlin, Gebr. Rasch
& Co., und Dumont, Bramsche, 1962
The Bauhaus Weimar-Dessau-Berlin-Chicago,
MIT Press, Cambridge, Massachusetts, 1969
    Marcel Franciscono:
*Walter Gropius and the creation of the Bauhaus in
Weimar—the ideals and artistic theories of its
founding years*, University of Illinois Press, Chicago
& London, 1971

Complete Bibliography

The American Association of Architectural Bibliog-
raphers: *Walter Gropius*, Papers, Vol. 111, The
University Press of Virginia, Charlottesville, 1966

1

HOUSING FOR FARM WORKERS, 1906
FARM SERVICE BUILDING, 1906
Janikow Estate, Dramburg, Pomerania
Architect: Walter Gropius
Client: Erich Gropius, Walter Gropius's uncle

2
FAGUS SHOE-LAST FACTORY, 1911
Alfeld, Germany
Architect: Walter Gropius with Adolf Meyer
Client: Karl Benscheidt

3

BENZENE MOTOR COACH, 1913
Designer: Walter Gropius
Client: Königsberg Locomotive Works

5
WERKBUND EXHIBITION MODEL FACTORY, 1914
(Office building, machine shop & pavilion)
Cologne, Germany
Architect: Walter Gropius with Adolf Meyer
Client: Der Deutsche Werkbund

9
CHICAGO TRIBUNE BUILDING, 1922
Chicago, Illinois
Competition Project
Architect: Walter Gropius with Adolf Meyer
Client: The Chicago Tribune

10

KALLENBACH RESIDENCE, 1922
Berlin, Germany
Project
Architect: Walter Gropius with Adolf Meyer
Client: Herr Kallenbach

12

MUNICIPAL THEATER, 1922
Jena, Germany
Architect: Walter Gropius with Adolf Meyer
Client: The City of Jena

SUMMER HOUSE BY THE BALTIC SEA, 1924
Project
Architect: Walter Gropius with Adolf Meyer
Client: Herr von Klitzing

THE BAUHAUS BUILDING, 1925
Dessau, Germany
Architect: Walter Gropius
Client: The City of Dessau

17
HOUSES FOR BAUHAUS FACULTY, 1925/26
Dessau, Germany
Architect: Walter Gropius
Client: The City of Dessau

TÖRTEN DEVELOPMENT, 1926/28
Dessau, Germany
Architect: Walter Gropius
Client: The City of Dessau

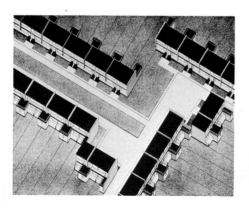

19
PREFABRICATED HOUSE FOR WERKBUND
HOUSING EXHIBITION, 1927
Stuttgart, Germany
Architect: Walter Gropius
Client: The City of Stuttgart

20
TOTAL THEATER, 1927
Berlin, Germany
Project
Architect: Walter Gropius
Client: Erwin Piscator

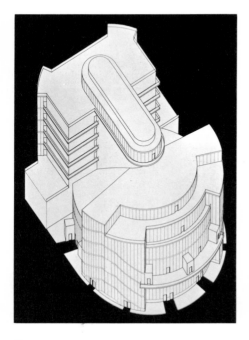

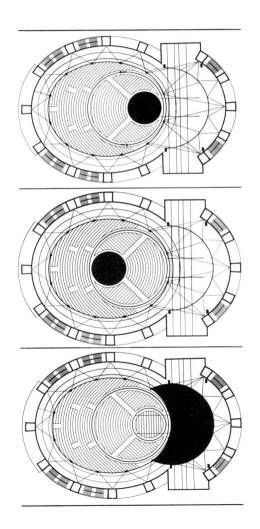

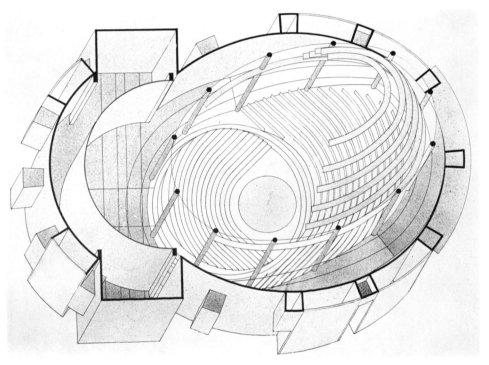

21
'STADTKRONE,' 1928
(Cultural and sports center)
Halle a.d. Saale, Germany
Project
Architect: Walter Gropius
Client: The City of Halle

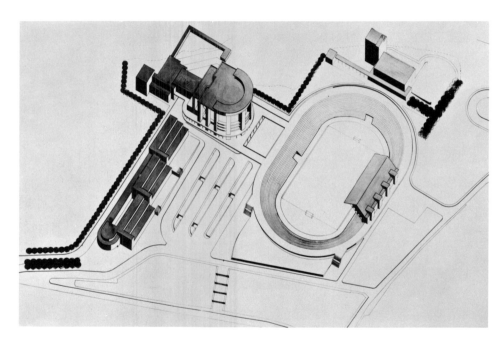

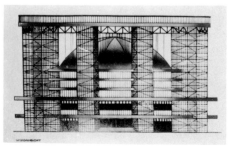

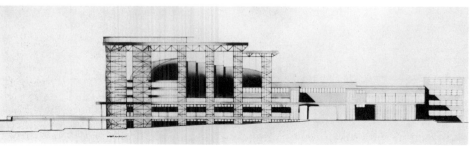

23
MUNICIPAL EMPLOYMENT OFFICE, 1927/28
Dessau, Germany
Architect: Walter Gropius
Client: The City of Dessau

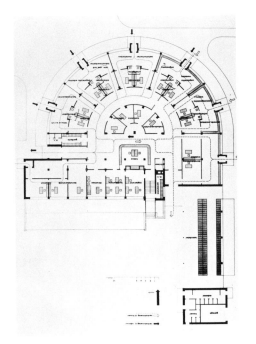

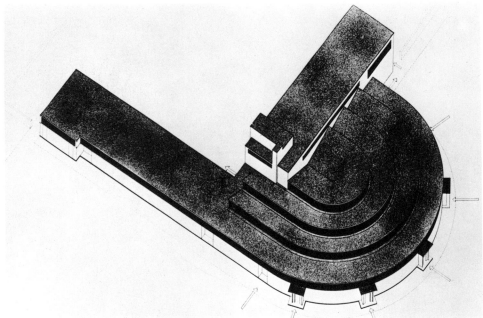

DAMMERSTOCK HOUSING DEVELOPMENT,
1927/28
Karlsruhe, Germany
Architect: Walter Gropius
Client: The City of Karlsruhe

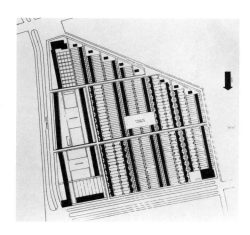

25
MODULAR FURNITURE UNITS, 1927/29
Designer: Walter Gropius
Client: Feder Stores, Berlin

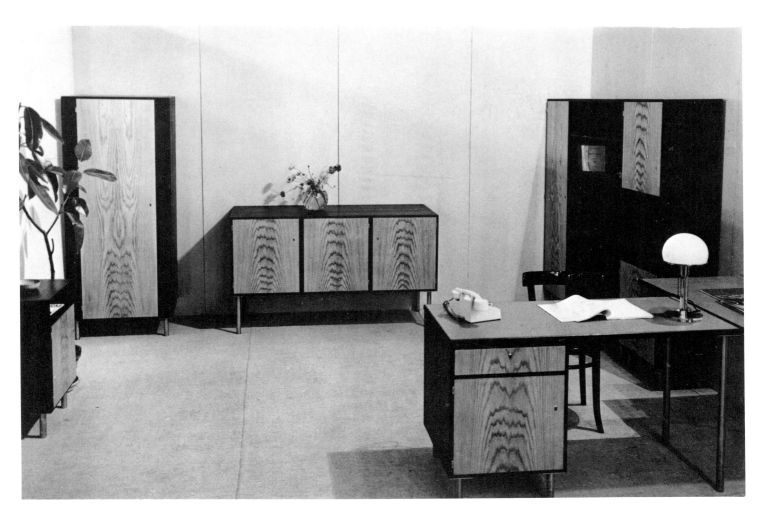

MEGASTRUCTURE, 1928
Project
Architect: Walter Gropius

SLAB APARTMENT BLOCK, 1929
Project
Architect: Walter Gropius

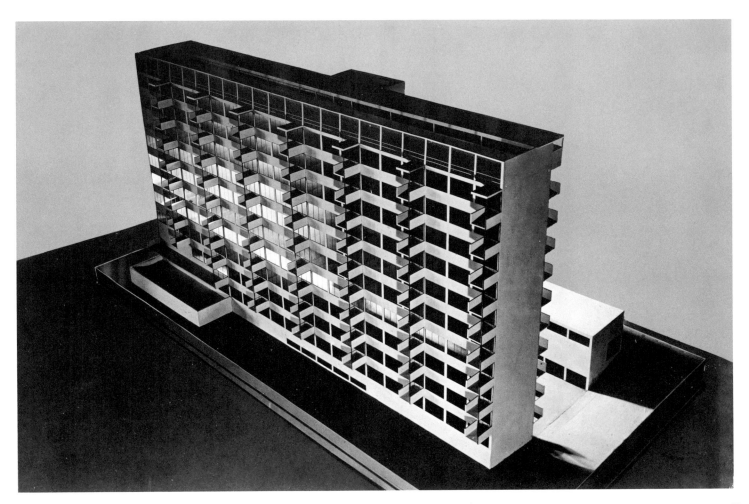

29

SIEMENSSTADT HOUSING DEVELOPMENT, 1929
Berlin, Germany
Architect: Walter Gropius
Engineer: Herr Mengeringhausen
Client: Cooperative Organization, Berlin

32

ADLER CABRIOLET, 1930
Designer: Walter Gropius
Client: Adler Automobile Works, Frankfurt/Main

34

UKRAINIAN STATE THEATER, 1930
Kharkov, Ukraine
Competition project
Architect: Walter Gropius
Client: The Ukrainian Soviet Socialist Republic

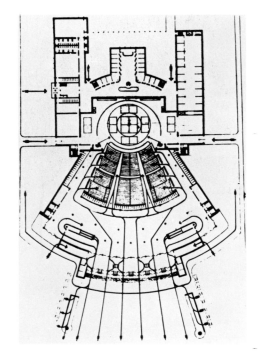

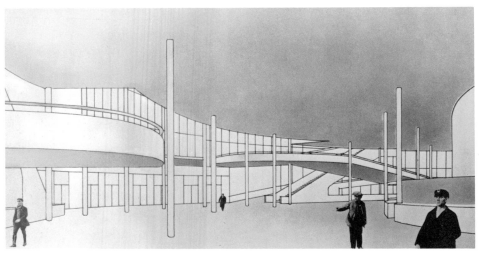

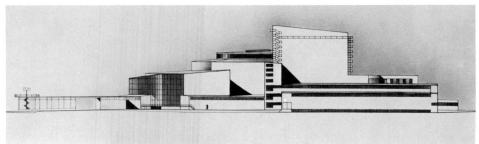

35
PREFABRICATED COPPER HOUSES, 1931
Finow, Germany
Architect: Walter Gropius
Client: Hirsch Kupfer und Messingwerke A.G.,
Berlin

36
SOVIET PALACE, 1931
Moscow, USSR
Competition project
Architect: Walter Gropius
Client: The Russian Embassy, Berlin

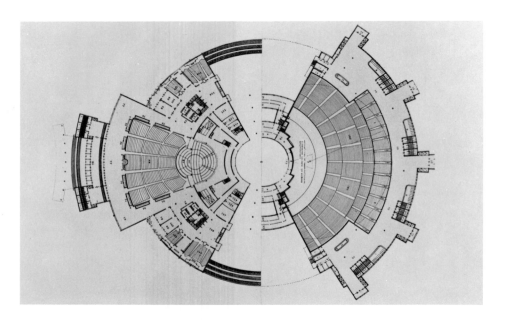

41
IMPINGTON VILLAGE COLLEGE, 1936
Cambridgeshire, England
Architects: Walter Gropius and Maxwell Fry
Client: Henry Morris, Secretary of the Educational
Committee of the County of Cambridge

43
GROPIUS RESIDENCE, 1937
Lincoln, Massachusetts
Architects: Walter Gropius and Marcel Breuer
Client: Mrs. James Storrow

44
HAGERTY RESIDENCE, 1938
Cohasset, Massachusetts
Architects: Walter Gropius and Marcel Breuer
Client: Mrs. Josephine Hagerty

CHAMBERLAIN RESIDENCE, 1939
Sudbury, Massachusetts
Architects: Walter Gropius and Marcel Breuer
Client: H. Chamberlain

47

FRANK RESIDENCE, 1939
Pittsburgh, Pennsylvania
Architects: Walter Gropius and Marcel Breuer
Client: Mr. Robert Frank

48

ALUMINUM CITY TERRACE HOUSING, 1941
New Kensington, near Pittsburgh, Pennsylvania
Architects: Walter Gropius and Marcel Breuer
Client: Federal Works Agency (FWA),
Division of Defense Housing

51
HARVARD GRADUATE CENTER, 1949
Cambridge, Massachusetts
Architect: TAC
Principals-in-charge: Walter Gropius, Norman C.
Fletcher, Louis A. McMillen, Ben Thompson
Client: Harvard University

53

INTERBAU APARTMENT BLOCK, 1956
Berlin, Germany
Architect: TAC
Principals-in-charge: Walter Gropius, Norman C.
Fletcher, H. Morse Payne
Contact Architect: Wils Ebert, Berlin
Client: The City of Berlin and Aktiengesellschaft
für den Aufbau des Hansaviertels

54

UNITED STATES EMBASSY, 1956/61
Athens, Greece
Architect: TAC
Principals-in-charge: Walter Gropius,
H. Morse Payne
Contact Architect: Perikles Sakellarios, Athens
Client: US State Department, Office of Foreign
Building Operations

THE UNIVERSITY OF BAGHDAD, 1957
Baghdad, Iraq
Architect: TAC
Principals-in-charge: Walter Gropius, Louis A.
McMillen, H. Morse Payne, Richard Brooker,
Peter W. Morton, Robert McMillan
Contact Architect: Hisham A. Munir & Associates,
Baghdad
Client: Government of the Republic of Iraq,
Ministry of Works and Housing

PAN AMERICAN WORLD AIRWAYS BUILDING,
1958/63
New York, NY
Architect: Emery Roth and Sons
Consulting Architects: Walter Gropius and
Pietro Belluschi
Client: Grand Central Building, Inc., New York

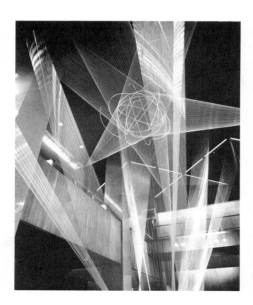

58

GROPIUSSTADT, 1959/71
Berlin-Buckow-Rudow, Germany
Architect: TAC
Principals-in-charge: Walter Gropius,
Alex Cvijanovic
Contact Architects: Wils Ebert, Hans Bandel, and
Heinz Viehrig, Berlin
Client: The City of Berlin

59

JOHN F. KENNEDY FEDERAL BUILDING, 1961/66
Boston, Massachusetts
Architects: TAC in association with Samuel
Glaser & Associates
TAC principals-in-charge: Walter Gropius,
Norman C. Fletcher
Client: US General Services Administration

60

COMBINED SCHOOL & DAY CARE CENTER,
1962/68
Gropiusstadt, Berlin, Germany
Architect: TAC
Principals-in-charge: Walter Gropius,
Alex Cvijanovic
Contact Architect: Wils Ebert, Berlin
Client: The Berlin Senate

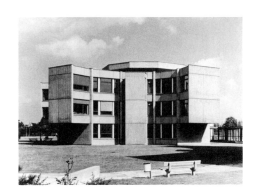

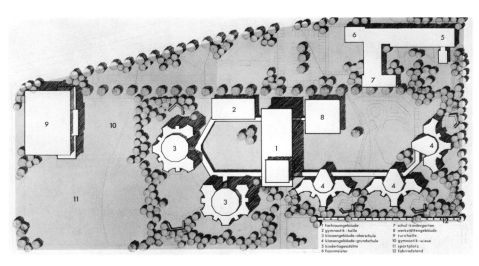

1 fachraumgebäude
2 gymnastik-halle
3 klassengebäude-oberschule
4 klassengebäude-grundschule
5 kindertagesstätte
6 hausmeister
7 schul-kindergarten
8 werkstättengebäude
9 turnhalle
10 gymnastik-wiese
11 sportplatz
12 fahrradstand

61
BAUHAUS ARCHIVE, 1964
Berlin, Germany
Architect: TAC
Principals-in-charge: Walter Gropius,
Alex Cvijanovic
Client: The City of Berlin

CHINA FACTORY "ROSENTHAL AM ROTBUHL",
1965/66
Selb, Germany
Architect: TAC
Principals-in-charge: Walter Gropius,
Alex Cvijanovic
Client: Rosenthal A.G., Selb

THOMAS GLASS FACTORY, 1968
Amberg, Germany
Architect: TAC
Principals-in-charge: Walter Gropius,
Alex Cvijanovic
Client: Rosenthal A.G., Amberg

66

CHINA TEA SET "TAC 1," 1968
CHINA COFFEE SET "TAC 2," 1968
Designer: TAC
Principals-in-charge: Walter Gropius,
Louis A. McMillen
Client: Rosenthal A.G., Selb

TOWER EAST OFFICE COMPLEX, 1968
Shaker Heights, Cleveland, Ohio
Architect: TAC
Principal-in-charge: Walter Gropius
Client: Central Cadillac Company, Cleveland

68
GERMAN AMBASSADOR'S RESIDENCE, 1968
Buenos Aires, Argentina
Project
Architect: TAC
Principals-in-charge: Walter Gropius,
Alex Cvijanovic
Contact Architect: Amancio Williams,
Buenos Aires
Client: The Federal Republic of Germany

The text for this catalog is set in Linofilm,
7 pt. Helvetica Light, 3 pt. leading between lines.
Heads are set in 7 pt. Helvetica Medium. Project
numbers and section titles are set in 12 pt. Helvetica
Light.

Text paper is 80 lb. Mohawk Superfine, High
Finish. Cover paper is 80 lb. Mohawk Superfine,
High Finish.